Killers

Killers

Britain's Deadliest Murderers
Tell Their Stories.

Kate Kray

JOHN BLAKE

Published by John Blake Publishing Ltd,
3 Bramber Court, 2 Bramber Road,
London W14 9PB, England

First published in hardback in 2002

ISBN 1 903402 49 2

British Library Cataloguing-in-Publication Data: A catalogue record for this
book is available from the British Library.

Design by ENVY

Printed and bound in Great Britain by
Creative Print and Design (Wales), Ebbw Vale, Gwent

1 3 5 7 9 10 8 6 4 2

Papers used by John Blake Publishing Ltd are natural, recyclable products
made from wood grown in sustainable forests. The manufacturing processes
conform to the environmental regulations of the country of origin.

Visit Kate Kray's web site at:
www.katekray.com

Contents

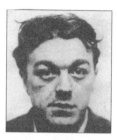

CHARLIE SMITH
219

RICHARD JOHN DENNICK
273

AVRIL GREGORY
247

SUE BUTTERWORTH
297

The Meaning of Life

Killers

It's like being on another planet ... that's the only way you can cope with it. I had to forget about my life before and think of it as being taken away from the world I had always known and put into another world. A world that was completely alien to me. A strange world of different noises, different smells. It's an unnatural world, a one-sex world and it's an unnatural life to be locked away 24 hours a day, every day. You know you're never going to be able to do simple things like swim in the sea or walk under the stars again. You know that from now on you don't think for yourself, or make any kind of decision for yourself, you're told what to do and when to do it. 'Please, Sir, can I do this? – please,

Sir, can I do that?' You know that's how it's going to be for the rest of your life – my life . ...If you can call it a life. I think it would have been kinder to hang me.

That was how one of the lifers I spoke to described his life sentence to me. I suppose in a way he was right. Now, every time I drive past a prison and see those high stone walls, I think of the prisoners who are kept there and think of it as just that – another world. A completely unnatural alien world. It doesn't take a genius to work out that if you lock a thousand men in one building for years on end it's going to be like an unexploded bomb just waiting to go off ...A world where a simple sausage can start a riot...

I was standing in line waiting to get my breakfast. There had been some delay in getting the hotplates on to the wing and the time allocated for breakfast was nearly over.

'Get a fucking move on,' one of the screws snapped as he shoved me hard in the back.

I fell against another con who was standing in front of me.

''Ere, watch what you're fucking doing,' he said. 'Look, you made me drop my sausage.' The half-cooked sausage rolled across the filthy floor, among the fag-ends. The con held out his small metal tray for another one.

The screw serving food said, 'Sorry that was the last one, there ain't any more sausages.'

A deathly silence fell along our line. 'Wot, no more

sausages!' someone gasped. 'I ain't having that — I'm entitled to a sausage and I want my fucking sausage and I want it now!'

The screws, leaning against the wall chatting, looked over and one snapped, 'Never mind about sausages, move along.' The con was determined, he banged his tray on the hotplate and shouted at the screw, 'I ain't fucking moving — I know my rights!'

Things were turning ugly and the screws started moving in. Crack!! The con who had lost his sausage turned and whacked a screw with his metal tray, breaking his nose. Quickly, alarm bells were pressed and an almighty fight broke out. The screws scrambled out of the wing as quickly as they could, locking us inside. We responded by barricading the doors and rampaging through the wing, smashing tables and chairs and anything else that got in our way. It was just sheer frustration bubbling out. It was like a shaken-up bottle of Coke and someone unscrewing the lid. The pressure was explosive! Nothing was going to stop the flow. We smashed everything we could lay our hands on. Nobody really knew why we were doing it. We just were. It felt good to be in control again, but it didn't last for long. We knew our new-found freedom would be short-lived and every one of us knew the consequences.

After a couple of hours, we had smashed all there was to smash and shouted all there was to shout. We had burnt ourselves out and none of us knew what to do next. We were all sitting around among the debris, smoking and chatting, when the governor appeared at one of the barricaded doors.

'All right, you've made your point, come out now and nobody gets hurt.'

Someone shouted, 'Go fuck yourself, you old git', and we all roared with laughter.

The governor shrugged his shoulders and gave the nod to the riot squad who were standing directly behind him. They looked like something out of a science fiction film, with their full facial helmets, big batons and riot shields. Believe me, they meant business. Within seconds they had stormed the wing and were kicking the shit out of us. We didn't stand a chance. Some of us ended up with broken noses, dislocated shoulders, cracked ribs, and the wing was completely destroyed. And all over a sausage ...

To you outside it probably sounds ridiculous, but that's how it is in prison. It's not the soft, cushy place that the media try to make out. It's a tough violent, brutal place. You have to fight every day — just to survive.

Christmas is the worst time. That's when you feel it the most. You miss your family so much the pain inside you cuts like a knife. Or when someone gets a 'Dear John' letter, which often happens with long-term prisoners. It affects the whole wing. You can't go and talk to your wife and sort it out; you just have to swallow and brood on it.

In writing this book, I spent many hours talking with lifers and they all seem to have the same look in their eyes — a look of despair and regret, a look that cries out: 'If only...'

Sitting, talking with them over a cup of tea in the visitors' hall, I often found it hard to believe that these people really had committed the horrific murders they were so calmly telling me about.

None showed much remorse for what they'd done, in as much as they were sorry and guilty for having stolen someone else's life, but they all regretted their crimes – because it meant a life in prison for themselves...

There's been a lot of political talk recently about life really meaning life, but the cons would argue that a life sentence already means just that. It stays with them until the day they die. It can never be revoked.

A life sentence is divided into four parts: security, training, assessment and, finally, preparation for release.

Prisoners are often moved from prison to prison. The authorities don't like them to get too settled and it is thought that too long in one prison can be detrimental for the lifer. Everyone needs stimulation and challenge and changing prisons at regular intervals can, they believe, help to provide this.

Stage One

Once they have been given a life sentence, all prisoners are allocated to what is known as a main centre prison. For men, that's currently Wormwood Scrubs in London, Gartree in Leicester, or Wakefield.

The small number of women lifers are usually sent to Durham H Wing, which is a small, secure unit that holds up to 40 women at a time. The unit is inside Durham men's prison. Or they are taken to Bullwood Hall in Essex.

The ever-increasing number of youngsters (under the

age of 21) serving a life sentence are sent to Aylesbury, Swinfen Hall and Castington. These main centres are lifer-only units and are meant to give the lifer a chance to settle down and come to terms with their offence and their sentence. It also gives the screws a chance to carry out an initial assessment and to decide if the prisoner is a risk to himself, other inmates or to staff.

After sentencing, you receive your tariff date. This is the length of time you must serve in order to meet what is called 'the punishment and deterrence' set by law. In all cases you must complete your tariff date before you're let out. However, your case will be looked at by the Local Review Committee before that, usually three years before your tariff date.

Tariff dates vary. My brother-in-law Reggie Kray, for example, didn't have a tariff date because he received a recommended sentence. The same is true of Harry Roberts. He has to serve a recommended 30 years, so the tariff system will not apply until he has completed his recommended sentence.

Stage Two

This is usually the longest part of the sentence and is mostly served in more than one prison. If you're considered a high-risk prisoner, then you are sent to a dispersal prison. These are the more secure prisons.

If not a high-risk prisoner, you are sent to a Category B training prison. These prisons have a more relaxed regime but still within a secure perimeter. Cat. B prisons are not only for lifers. Other inmates will be serving much shorter sentences. These men will all have a release date and may be allowed parole and home leave. This can cause problems for the lifers. They often strike up a close friendship with these other inmates, so they find their departure hard to take. That, in turn, can cause frustration and resentment – and sometimes trouble.

Stage Three

After many years in a Cat. B prison, the move to a Category C is normally the most difficult. For a long time the lifer has probably been looking forward to the day when he will eventually be moved to a Cat. C, because, as he sees it, he's finally on his way out. It is a big step forward.

Cat. Cs are much less secure and have a lower level of supervision, although still within a secure perimeter. However, the lifer can face new problems. The inmate population will be a lot younger than most lifers at this stage in their sentence and they tend to be serving much shorter sentences. In a Cat. C prison, the lifer is expected to adjust to the pressures and stresses of life on the outside. He also loses all the privileges that he has become accustomed to in other prisons, while release is still an uncertainty. He sees other Cat. C prisoners enjoying home leave and looking forward to their release date but the wait for the lifer is endless. He still has to undergo many reviews and reports before there is even the prospect of a move to a Cat. D.

Stage Four: Category D, release phase and PRES hostel.

Under no circumstances can a lifer proceed to a Cat. D without the approval of the Minister of State for Prisons, and that's only given after a recommendation from the Parole Board.

After settling in to a Cat. D prison, the lifer may be taken on supervised days out. These become more and more frequent, until the lifer has built up confidence and trust. Then, and only then, is he allowed unsupervised days out and allowed to work outside the prison.

Security at Cat. Ds is kept to a minimum and, essentially, the lifer is his own gaoler. After a specified number of days out without any problems, and when all the reports have been satisfactory, the Parole Board and the Home Secretary eventually agree that the lifer can be given a provisional release date.

This is usually preceded by a period of six to nine months at a Pre-Release Employment Scheme hostel (PRES). While he's at the hostel, the lifer is expected to find a job and will have to save the best part of his wage to show that he can cope on the outside. Once he has complied with all the rules, and only with approval, he will be allowed weekend home leave.

Stage Five: life licence.
After many years in prison, and only after long consideration by the Parole Board, a lifer may eventually be allowed out of prison for good. This will be on licence and under the strict supervision of the Probation Office. However, the final decision to release a lifer does not come from the Parole Board; they can only submit a

recommendation for release. The final word comes from the Home Secretary.

If, and when, you're finally let out on licence, you are still not free in one sense. You have to report to a probation officer once, maybe twice, a week in the beginning. You also have to ask their permission to do anything like move house or change your job. You can't go abroad on holiday or have any association with known criminals.

If you are lucky enough to find a job, your probation officer may insist that you inform your employer that you're 'out on licence'. In some cases, if the crime you committed was a particularly violent one, you may have to tell the employer the nature of the crime: then it's up to him if he still wants to employ you. If, as a lifer, you start to become personally or romantically involved with someone, your probation officer will want to meet the person and, if you haven't already told them that you are 'out on licence', the probation officer will.

A detailed report on your progress is sent to the Home Office every three months. If your probation officer or the Home Office is not happy with your progress, you can be recalled to prison at any time.

For this book, I interviewed ten lifers. All of their stories are different. Some are sad; some are just downright brutal. I didn't write this book to justify or condone in any way what they did nor to say that they shouldn't be punished for their horrific crimes. On the contrary, I don't think murder should go unpunished. What interested me was the truth – as they saw it – of what happened – not the newspaper stories or the gossip but the real story behind the story. I don't think it's my job to judge them – they've been judged already. All I am trying to do here is tell you their stories as they told them to me.

It was my brother-in-law Reggie Kray who first introduced me to Harry Roberts in Gartree Prison in 1988. When he was interviewed for this book Harry had been in prison for 28 years for killing three policemen but, in all, he spent 33 years and seven months of his 58-year life in some of the toughest prisons in Britain, although to see and speak to him, you wouldn't think it.

Harry is a very intelligent, astute man who keeps himself up to date with the outside world in every aspect. After serving so much time in prison, though, there isn't anything he doesn't know about the system. He says: 'Don't matter how much you "hoot and holler", you will never beat the system.'

If anybody should know, Harry Roberts should – he's an expert. Harry first went to prison in 1954, before I was even born, when prisons were tough. He told me that back in the 1950s prisoners weren't allowed to talk, and a deathly silence hung over the cold, wrought-iron landings. In those days the food was slop; you were only allowed one egg a year, at Easter, and your one treat was Christmas Day when there was fish and chips for dinner.

'They didn't muck about with ya in those days,' he told me. 'They would birch ya or give ya the cat-o'-nine-tails or, if ya murdered someone, they would simply hang ya!'

Harry has the dubious honour of being Britain's

longest-serving Category A prisoner. Being a Cat. A prisoner for more than 20 years means that Harry was considered a high risk and treated accordingly. He was monitored 24 hours a day, something which not only affects the prisoner but also his family and friends. For instance, if someone wants to visit a Cat. A prisoner, the prisoner must first ask their wing officer for an application form so that the visitor can be included in their list of approved visitors. The visitor must fill in their full name, address, occupation, phone number and relationship – if they are not a relative then they will have to state how and when they came to know the prisoner. The Governor will then write and ask if the person wishes to visit and the visitor will have to send two passport-sized photographs to the prison. Once the prison has received them, they will ask the police to go to the visitor's house and check that the photographs are valid. After all that, and for security reasons, visits with Cat. A prisoners take place in a separate room, in the presence of two officers.

At Broadmoor and Rampton security is slightly different. The forms are still sent to the visitor's home and still have to be approved by the Home Office, but the photographs are taken at the hospital. All the visitor's personal information is then put on a special card, a bit like a credit card. After that, each time a visit is made, the visitor must produce the card or entry will be refused.

In 1992, card phones were introduced in most category prisons. Using their earnings or private cash, prisoners are allowed to buy these special Prison Service phone cards from the prison canteen. Of course, for lifers who have been locked away for a long time these new card phones were amazing! Ordinary phone cards are no use as prison phones don't take them, nor in-coming calls for that matter.

In most prisons, phone calls are only occasionally listened in to by the screws, and this is done at random. If you are Cat. A, however, the calls are always listened to and are also sometimes tape recorded. Cat. A prisoners may only call a telephone number on their approved list, once again only after stringent checks have been made, and all Cat. A calls have to be pre-booked.

The governor of each prison sets a limit on how much a prisoner can spend each month on phone calls and prisoners are normally only allowed to buy two phone cards at one time, but this does vary from prison to prison.

In all the years Harry Roberts has been inside, he's tried to escape – and failed – 22 times. That's why I was very embarrassed when, on one of my visits to Harry, I took him a present. I had asked Harry if there was anything I could get for him and he had said that he would like a track suit – large size and preferably a dark colour like navy blue or black.

I searched high and low for a plain track suit and couldn't find one but I did find a really great navy blue track suit with a broad yellow stripe down the arms and legs. Harry was very grateful. When he took it out of the bag in the visitors' hall, however, he howled with laughter. 'It's a fucking escapee's track suit!' he said. Only then did I remember that prisoners who persist in trying to escape are made to wear a suit with wide yellow stripes down the side, presumably so that the screws can spot them easily, especially if they're clambering over the wall!

I offered to change it but Harry wouldn't hear of it. Even so, I've never seen him actually wearing it!

Harry helped me a lot in writing this book. It was while Harry was in Long Lartin Prison, that he introduced me to Colin Richards.

I had just finished writing Harry's chapter when he phoned and asked me if I needed anyone else for this book. He sounded upset and that wasn't like Harry who is normally so cheerful. I asked him what was wrong.

'I thought I had problems,' he said. 'Well, I've just come out of the cell of a bloke here who's in a wheelchair. Problems! I don't know the meaning of the word!' Harry explained to me how bad it was for Colin – he said he couldn't even turn his wheelchair around in his cell. 'He can't go to the TV room because it's on the top landing.' Harry said it was bad enough spending the rest of your life in prison but to be in a wheelchair and still be a lifer was a nightmare.

Harry told Colin about my book but at first he didn't want to take part. He had been in prison for ten years and had been suffering from deep depression so he didn't want to talk to anyone. A week afterwards, he changed his mind. Later, he told me that the only reason he had agreed to talk to me was that for the ten years he had been away he had always had the same number sewn into his property – 394 – and he thought that maybe, in the third month of 1994, things might change for him. It must have been fate because

Harry Roberts was at a different prison at the time and was only moved to the same prison as Colin for one month, the third month of 1994. If Harry hadn't moved, I would never have met Colin. So maybe there was something in Colin's prediction – who knows?

My journey to Long Lartin Prison in Evesham was a nightmare, after three of my trains were cancelled. Eventually, I met Colin Richards on a cold, wet afternoon in March 1994, and that visit will always stay with me.

Patiently, I waited for prison wardens to bring Colin into the small, grubby visitors' hall. Harry Roberts joined us and we all had tea and chocolate biscuits. Colin is a big man with a bushy beard and looks like a Vietnam vet. At first he was quiet and shy and found it hard to talk about his crime and his own appalling injuries.

Harry had told me about Colin but I wasn't prepared for what I found. Colin seemed such a sad, lonely figure, his eyes full of regret and despair. He's a paraplegic, paralysed from the chest down. Until then, I didn't know there were any disabled people in prison but there are, and Colin Richards is one of them.

Having had some experience with disabled people, I am aware of many of the difficulties that they face every day of their lives but Colin's difficulties are tenfold. He confided many things on our visits but one of the most poignant was just horrible.

He explained to me that one of the worst things about being a paraplegic, other than not being able to walk, was the difficulty of not being able to go to the toilet. Instead, he has to evacuate his bowels by hand. When he wants to go for a pee, he has to insert a small plastic tube down his penis – a terrible thing to have to do by anyone's standards. For Colin, this unenviable task was made much worse.

While he was in Parkhurst Prison on the Isle of Wight, the rubber gloves and plastic tubes that Colin needed were denied to him. He was told that he was only allowed five a week, while he needs five a day! When he asked why, he was told: 'We will not give you any more plastic tubes in case you hang yourself with them!' Colin pleaded with the authorities and tried to explain that he really did need the tubes and rubber gloves. In the end the authorities gave in and said that he could have 'new for old'. Colin must hand in his used tubes and gloves and then he can be issued with new ones.

Colin's cell was 12 feet by 7 feet, just big enough for his wheelchair. He is not able to turn his wheelchair around nor move it about. There are no handrails fitted in the cell but every day Colin is expected to drag himself in and out of bed.

The communal TV room is situated on the top landing, which makes it impossible for Colin ever to watch TV. All he has to take away the boredom is his small radio. At one time, a friendly inmate would carry Colin on his back up the iron steps to the TV room but the screws stopped this. They said that it couldn't be allowed in case the inmate dropped Colin, because the prison authorities were not insured for such an accident.

That goes for the screws too. They are not supposed to

lift Colin in case they injure their backs. That's fair enough; Colin is a big man and very heavy and the screws shouldn't have to risk injury by pulling him in and out of his wheelchair. But Colin needs help. If the inmates aren't allowed to help, and the screws can't or won't help, who the hell will?

On one of my visits to Colin, he told me that the National Health Service does not apply to prisoners. While you're in prison, your health care is the responsibility of the Health Care Service. Prisons are allocated a sum of money for health care each year. When the money runs out, so does the dental and medical care.

When they first go into prison, all prisoners undergo a medical examination in the reception. Medical records only follow you into prison if the medical officer decides that there is a good reason for having them sent. Unless you tell the medical officer of any health problems you have, he won't know about your ailments, so you may not get any treatment for them. In general, he will ask you if you have been receiving any medical or psychiatric treatment, if you have had any problems with alcohol or drugs and also whether you have HIV (the AIDS virus) or if you have had contact with anyone with HIV.

The physical side of Colin Richards's problems is obvious but the mental problems he is suffering run much deeper. I feel very strongly about Colin's situation. The crime that he committed was an appalling one, as you will find out when you read his chapter. However, the medieval days of throwing a prisoner into a dungeon and letting him rot are long gone. As a civilised nation, we would be appalled if an animal was being treated in this way. Colin Richards is a human being and should be entitled to human dignity. He has nobody. Soon after he was sentenced his wife left him and now lives in France with the two children he adores. Since he's been away, both of his parents have died. He has nobody to care for him nor to help him; every day of his life is a struggle.

He told me about a visit that he had recently. His visitor had travelled a long way for the two-hour visit. It had taken Colin all morning to get ready and there were only three-quarters of an hour left of the visit but still nobody had come to help him across to the visiting hall where his visitor was waiting. By the time he finally reached the five steep steps leading into the hall, he had had enough. Still, no one came to help him. The hall was packed with cons and their visitors. Nobody looked up or gave him a second glance.

'It felt like I was invisible,' he said. 'The door behind me was locked. I couldn't go back and I couldn't go down the steps. I just sat there unable to move. In sheer desperation, I cried out: "Please, somebody help me!"

'The whole of the visiting hall fell silent. Tears rolled down my face. I was helpless. I just sat at the top of those steps and cried. At that moment I just wished I was dead!' His eyes filled with tears as he spoke and he dropped his head.

I didn't know what to say to him. Normally I am never stuck for words but, for the first time in my life, I struggled to find the right words to say, to give him some kind of hope.

'There must be something someone can do.' I told him.

He looked at me and sighed: 'Oh yeah, what?'

As I left the prison that wet afternoon, I promised that I would find out what could be done to help him. All the way home on the train, I couldn't get Colin out of my mind. There had to be some kind of help available, but what? I didn't know where to start.

When I got home I looked up a booklet written by the Howard League for Penal Reform. There, they list all the organisations that are useful to people in prison. As I thumbed through the pages, I found that there were groups and counselling services to help just about everyone – there is a Rastafarian Advisory service, a Gay Rights action group – in all, over 66 different organisations. To my surprise, there was nothing for disabled people in prison. In the ten years that Colin has been in prison, he has never had any counselling to help him to come to terms with his disability. Surely, I thought, in the new prisons that are being built in this country, they can build some kind of secure unit with facilities to cater for the likes of Colin Richards.

I promised Colin that I would try to help him – not to campaign for his release but to make the public aware of what was happening, and continues to happen, to people like him.

Most of us are unaware that there are people with disabilities in prison, just as most people think there is only one women's prison in Britain – Holloway in London. In fact, there are 12 in England and Wales. Holloway Prison provides a national centre for treating women with psychiatric problems. Styal Prison, which is in Cheshire, Cookham Wood in Kent and Bullwood Hall in Essex are all closed prisons for convicted and sentenced women prisoners. The only other closed prison for women is H Wing at Durham and that is where I visited most of the women in this book.

Durham H Wing is a small unit inside Durham men's prison. The self-contained unit holds up to 40 women, all serving long sentences, and most are classified Cat. A. Women are allowed to wear their own clothes as long as they're considered to be suitable. However, there are many other things that have to be taken into account when you're a female prisoner. If you're pregnant and likely to give birth shortly after your arrest or committal, you will go to one of the three mother and baby units that exist at Holloway, Styal and Askham Grange.

According to prison rules, pregnant women prisoners should not be alone at night; they must share a cell or have a bed in the hospital wing so that there are other people around to call on for help if necessary. If you give birth while you are in prison, or if you have a very young baby when you are sent to prison, you can apply to have your baby with you. The mother and baby unit at Holloway takes babies up to nine months. At Styal closed prison and Askham Grange open prison, the age limit is 18 months.

If you apply to keep your baby with you in prison, your application will be considered very carefully by a team of doctors, health visitors, paediatricians, prison staff and Social

Services. They will consider different factors:

a) if your other children were in care before you were
   sent to prison;
b) whether your baby will be over the unit age limit
   before your release;
c) if you're suffering from a mental or physical illness
   that will affect your ability to look after your baby;
d) if you are considered a disruptive influence and will
   not co-operate with staff.

Once you have been accepted into the unit there are, of
course, strict rules and they must be followed.

The way each unit is run varies but there are rules about
not having your baby in your bed and about when you're
allowed to bath a baby. Babies are usually left in a nursery
for at least four hours a day while the prisoner is at work or
in a class.

Depending on your behaviour, the Prison Service can
decide to move you to another prison. This could mean
heartbreaking separation for you and your baby. If, for
instance, you are at Askham Grange and your baby is 12
months old and you were then sent to Holloway, your baby
would be over the unit age limit and the baby would have
to go somewhere else. There are special visiting
arrangements for children who are not in prison with their
mothers. They can be brought in for fortnightly visits. These
visits are extended and much more relaxed than other visits
but the prisoners find it difficult and become frustrated.

The overwhelming need to mother their children can sometimes be the cause of trouble inside women's prisons. Linda Calvey, who I met in Durham H wing, told me: 'It really gets to the women, being separated from their kids. It wasn't so bad for me because mine were a bit older. But not being there for them if they have a problem; knowing someone else is looking after your kids, is the worst. You feel helpless!'

When I met Linda, she hadn't long become a grandmother and she proudly showed me photographs of her grand-daughter. Prison is not the sort of place you expect to find a grandma and Linda Calvey certainly doesn't look anything like one. When I visited her, she looked young, was dressed in trendy clothes and was planning to remarry.

Over 80,000 offences against prison discipline are punished by the authorities each year. A high level of these tend to be in young offender institutions and women's prisons.

Many of the long-term prisoners to whom I have spoken tell me that the thing that gets under their skin most is the stupid rules in prison. These rules often don't make any sense to the prisoner and they find themselves getting in trouble for what seems to them just a screw having 'an attitude'. Take, for instance, the rules about shaving. Men are expected to shave daily, unless they already had a beard when they were arrested. If you want to grow a beard or a moustache or to shave one off, you have to make out an application to the governor. While this may seem a stupid rule to the prisoner, when I asked a prison officer the reason for it he said it was simple: 'In case the prisoner escapes! Every year prisoners have an up-to-date photo taken of them, to be issued to the police if they were to escape. If they had grown a beard inside prison then nobody would recognise them.'

Prison discipline is a big part of prison life. If a prisoner commits an offence while in prison, the first thing that happens is that he or she is put on report. The forms are handed to the governor and the prisoner will have to report to him. If he is found guilty of the offence, then the governor can hand out a variety of punishments:

a) a caution;
b) loss of privileges for up to 28 days (14 for prisoners under 21);
c) stoppage of up to 28 days' earnings (14 for prisoners under 21);
d) confinement for up to three days;
e) up to an additional 28 days in custody;
f) exclusion from work for up to 14 days;

If these punishments are not considered to have worked, there are other control measures, like confiscation of property and Rule 43.

Rule 43 means that you are kept in solitary confinement, separated from the main wing of the prison, and have a different regime from other prisoners. There are two types of Rule 43 prisoners. The system is sometimes used to give a violent man a 'cooling off' period, generally known as GOAD (good order and discipline), or is sometimes used for a prisoner who could be a target for physical attacks, such as a child killer.

Alternatively, a prisoner could be transferred to another prison under the order of GOAD. Once all of these measures have been tried and have failed, and if the prisoner is violent, the governor can order that he is:

a) temporarily confined in a special, unfurnished cell called 'special accommodation';
b) placed in a mechanical restraint, i.e.:
  – a body belt (with iron cuffs for male prisoners and leather cuffs for female prisoners);
  – handcuffs (male prisoners);
  – leather wrist straps (female prisoners).

These tough measures are only used if the governor feels they are necessary to prevent the prisoner from injuring himself or others. If a prisoner being moved from one part of the prison to another kicks out, ankle straps can also be used to restrain him.

If the medical officer thinks the prisoner poses a danger to himself or to staff, he can order him to be held in a protective cell or placed in a loose, canvas restraint jacket (straight jacket).

Prisoners quickly become versed in all these rules and punishments and few behave so badly that they have to be used. Lifers, especially, learn to 'play the system', as they call it. Many I met were involved in disputes with the prison authorities over what they see as their rights. In fact, I think some prisoners probably know more about the law and prison rules than the Home Secretary does! I'm sure, too, that fighting the system is one of the things that keep many prisoners going. Few are better at playing the system than Jim Dowsett who tells his story in this book.

Jim is forever fighting for his rights. When I met him he was busy suing a prison officer after a row and also writing to the Crown Prosecution Service to order the Suffolk police to return all the paperwork they took from his office after his arrest. Jim was serving his sentence in Whitmoor High Security Prison in March, Cambridgeshire. I met him through a friend, Joey Pyle, who was serving time in the same prison. Joey gets on well with Jim because they're both businessmen, so I suppose they speak the same language.

Jim duly rang me and I promised to visit. I asked him if there was anything he'd like me to bring up for him and he said, 'Saucepans'. Apparently the prison was allowing Joey and Jim to cook some of their own meals. So I popped into Woolworth's on the way and bought three non-stick pans.

As prisons go, Whitmoor is better than most because it's modern. Security is very tight. You are thoroughly searched as you go in, checked with metal detectors and there are plenty of security cameras around. However, the visiting hall is carpeted and, instead of the usual school chairs and Formica-topped tables, there are low easy chairs and coffee tables. There is even a play area in the corner so that the prisoners can get to see their children.

The hall is vast, like a big aeroplane hanger. Mainstream prisoners sit on one side and the 'nonces and ponces' (rapists and child molesters) on the other, separated by a gangway and prison officers. This is the only time that the two groups of criminals get close to each other.

At the back of the hall, separated by a wall, are the Cat. A high-risk prisoners.

I'd seen photos of Jim in newspaper cuttings but when I met him, he looked much older than his 48 years. That's what prison does to some people – it ages them inside and out.

Avril Gregory was 20 years old when I first visited her. She is beautiful, just like a china doll. She looks naive and sort of lost. When she talks, there's none of the usual enthusiasm of youth. She speaks dully. I met Avril through Linda Calvey in the H Wing at Durham Prison. I asked her if she wanted to be a chapter in my book and she said she would have to ask her mum. A few days later a letter arrived saying her mum said it was all right. Unlike a lot of prisoners, Avril was glad to tell me her story and was completely honest. She never once tried to evade any questions nor to bend the truth. She told me exactly how it was. While I was writing her story, I felt sad that such a young girl could end up serving life. Parts of her story made me cry. But when she told me that she went looking for the boy who was killed with two knives, a pickaxe handle and a cosh, I couldn't believe my ears.

Avril told me:

I know what happened was terrible and I know I had to go to prison. I expected to be punished. But I didn't kill Scott Beaumont. I was just there at the time it happened.

When we all went out on that Friday night, never for one moment did we ever intend for anyone to be killed. We were just kids and when you're young you're just stupid. You just don't think of the consequences of what you're doing. That's why I wanted to tell my story – so if there is a young tearaway reading this, they might stop and think before they do anything stupid. Before it's too late. It's too late for me – I've ruined my life. I know I will always be known as a murderer and a lifer...

A new scheme has been set up to help constantly reoffending youngsters in Nottingham, some as young as 15. The court sends them in groups into Nottingham Prison. There, lifers such as Harry Roberts take them on a tour around the prison and show them what prison is really like. The youngsters are handcuffed and locked in a cell. Then lifers talk to the kids at street level, telling them that it's not 'big' to be in prison, that it doesn't matter what anyone tells them – it's shit being inside.

Recently, I went to visit Harry Roberts in Nottingham Prison. He told me that the day before he had been showing a group of youngsters around. He said:

We were walking across the exercise yard, chatting to the kids, showing them around. One of them had just expressed his greatest fear of prison, asking if it was true that boys are

raped in jail. Just at that moment a big black man called
out:
' 'Ere, Harry, save one of those for me!'
The big fella was only larking about but it scared the boys
half to death — they couldn't have been any older than 15.
When they left the prison, one of the boys came up to me
and said that he is never going to get in trouble again,
because he never wants to go to prison.

The longest-serving prisoner in Britain is the triple child-killer John Straffen. It was in 1951 that the name Straffen first caused nationwide revulsion. He was sent to Broadmoor for strangling six-year-old Brenda Goddard and her friend Cicely Batstone, aged nine, near Bath.

Seven months later he escaped from Broadmoor. After just four hours of freedom, he strangled his third victim, five-year-old Linda Bowyer. This time he was sentenced to death but reprieved from the gallows just five days before his execution date. The sentence was commuted to life imprisonment. Doctors declared that he had a mental age of nine. At his trial the judge said: 'You might just as well try a babe in arms.'

He's been in prison ever since and is currently in Long Lartin Prison in Evesham, Worcestershire. Over 43 years of incarceration have done nothing to rid John Straffen of the terrible burden he carries with him of his shocking crimes. His eyes are narrowed and blank. Twice he has been turned down for parole and it is doubtful whether he will ever be released. He is a lonely figure just waiting to die.

Many of the people I've met while writing this book, like Colin Richards and Avril Gregory, have been sad and, after meeting them, you feel very low – their sadness is contagious. I think the Nottingham scheme for youngsters is a great idea. Let them see sad figures like John Straffen so that they can decide for themselves that they'll never end up like that. Let them see the cells. After visiting so many prisons while researching for this book I can tell you that what I've seen has convinced me to stay forever on the straight and narrow.

The worst place I visited was Rampton, when I went to see Richard Dennick. Rampton Hospital is a deceiving place. On the outside it has the look of a military barracks but, once inside, it has the coldness of a Victorian asylum. The long corridors seem to wind for miles. It's like a rabbit warren. On the walls hang paintings done by the inmates, and down each side of the corridors are big, bolted doors, behind which are the patients.

I was taken into the depths of Rampton, to Concord Ward, to see Richard Dennick. The thing that struck me was the cold emptiness of the place. I had visited my husband Ron at Broadmoor but it was nothing like Rampton.

A burly officer unlocked the heavy steel door leading into Concord Ward. As I stepped in, there was a stale smell of confinement.

Every home has its own individual smell but Concord Ward has its own pungent odour, created by 16 men living in a closed environment. The sickening smell is a mixture of stewed tea, tobacco and body odour. The whitewashed walls are stained brownish-yellow from years of cigarette smoke. It looked like a geriatric ward in a general hospital. The big, swinging doors leading into the dorm were open and rows of unmade beds stood on either side. At the end was a room with a small glass window. I peered in. The room was empty apart from a bed; on the door was a big brass lock. It must be where the patients are put if they get 'upset'.

I was led into a small dining room alongside the kitchen. Under the watchful eye of a screw, Ricky unlocked the fridge to get the milk. I sat down at the table. A small vase of artificial flowers stood on the tea-stained gingham tablecloth. As he started to talk, Ricky poured the piping hot tea. Like young Avril, his voice seemed flat and dull. Not surprising for a 27-year-old man who was given a life sentence at the age of 15.

He has grown from boy to man inside. The crime that Ricky committed was terrible. He killed a vicar in a vicious, brutal attack. In his chapter, Ricky talks openly about the attack and leaves nothing out. After all these years, he still thinks he was right to kill him. He said that, in court, they portrayed the killing as done for pure gain. Ricky explained with anger that they wasn't interested that the vicar, a pillar of society, had died trying to abuse him. 'Oh no, they didn't want to hear about that,' he said.

I was very struck by how different Rampton is from Broadmoor. I know Broadmoor well from visiting my husband Ronnie and my brother-in-law Charlie Smith who married my sister Maggie.

I had been visiting Ron for a few months when he told me about young Charlie who was on the same ward as Ron, called Somerset Ward. Ron asked me if I had a friend who would visit Charlie. My sister had just left her husband and was staying with me. I said I would ask her. The very next day she made the long trip up to visit Charlie Smith. Little did we know that that visit would lead to marriage.

Charlie was 35 years old. He had never really known anything other than life in an institution of one kind or another. He was even born in a prison. After a traumatic childhood filled with abuse, he killed for the first time at the age of 17, then again in prison, and was sent to Broadmoor indefinitely.

Eighteen years later he met Maggie and things changed for him. He went out on shopping trips and on a day visit home – under escort, of course – before applying to be transferred to the Trevor Gibbons unit at Maidstone psychiatric hospital. However, these things take time. For Maggie, as well as Charlie, it will be a long wait.

All the lifers in this book have very different stories to tell. I was very aware when I was writing it that some people think such criminals shouldn't have the opportunity to tell their stories at all, for fear that they will glamorize their crime and, of course, themselves. These people will say, 'What about the victims? These murderers may be spending their lives in prison but at least they're still alive, unlike their victims.'

I do know, or at least I can imagine, that this is hard to take, especially for the families who lost someone they loved through someone else's act of violence. But we can't pretend that these people don't exist. They do. They made the headlines, they were found guilty of murder and, quite rightly, they have been locked up. However, after talking to so many lifers and hearing their stories, I don't think that murder should carry a mandatory life sentence. I do think that if you commit murder you should go to prison, but I think that each case should be judged on its own merits. Take the case of young Avril. She should have been punished – she admits that – but not with a life sentence.

In her chapter she openly admits taking the knives that killed the boy, but she didn't kill him. Someone else did. Ricky, too, should be punished for what he did, but doesn't the fact that the vicar tried to abuse him count for anything? He was a young, impressionable boy who hadn't even discovered his own sexuality. The 64-year-old vicar was a man of the cloth – a man to look up to. Ricky was confused – and still is.

In a strange twist of fate, these lifers have become victims themselves. I haven't set out to glamorize them or excuse their crime in any way and I haven't made heroes of them. They're not heroes. However, this is probably the first time they've told their own stories in their own way and in their own words. If you read their stories, it makes it easier to understand how such terrible things can happen. Surely, that's no bad thing.

John
Straffen

Killers

It was a cold, grey November day; the early morning air was freezing. The thin, chilling rain was still falling as I parked my car in the visitor's bay. I pulled my collar up, ducked my head down against the icy drizzle and walked towards the prison. I had come to Long Lartin high-security jail in Evesham, Worcester, to visit Europe's longest-serving prisoner – John Thomas Straffen.

It was in 1951 – Winston Churchill was Prime Minister and the scars of the Second World War were still evident – when the name Straffen first caused nationwide revolution. In July of that year, Straffen came across a little girl named Brenda Goddard, aged six, in a field and offered to show her where to find some flowers. It was there that he strangled her.

On 8 August the same year, he strangled Cicely Batstone aged nine.

At Winchester Assizes, doctors declared that Straffen, then aged 21, had a mental age of nine, and was found unfit to stand trial for the double murder and was subsequently sent to Broadmoor Hospital for the Criminally Insane.

Seven months later, he escaped from Broadmoor. He gave the guards the slip, climbed on to a shed and scaled a wall to freedom. After just four hours on the outside, he murdered his third victim, five-year-old Linda Bowyer. Linda was found strangled in a wood near her home at Farley Hill, ten miles from Broadmoor. This time, Straffen was deemed fit to stand trial and was sentenced to death by Mr Justice Cassels, but reprieved from the gallows just five days before his execution by the then Home Secretary, who advised the Queen to exercise her prerogative of mercy.

The sentence was commuted to life imprisonment. The judge at his trial said, 'You might just as well try a babe in arms.'

Straffen has been imprisoned since 1951 making him the longest-serving 'lifer' in Britain and Europe.

As I waited in the visiting centre prior to meeting John Straffen, I thought about his crime and felt somewhat apprehensive and doubtful about visiting a child murderer. I admit that, after reading the newspapers and watching news bulletins about a child being killed, I, too, stand up and shout, 'Lock 'em up and throw away the key,' and that's the last I think about it. But what happens to offenders after they have been sentenced? Capital punishment has been abolished and we no longer live in the Dark Ages when convicted killers were locked in dungeons. Nor do they fall off the face of the earth; they do exist, and burying our heads in the sand doesn't make them disappear.

In John Straffen's case, society did just that — locked him up and threw away the key. After more than 49 years in prison, he is still a Category A high-risk prisoner and for such prisoners security is tight, even tighter than when I visited my husband Ronnie Kray in Broadmoor.

I felt like I was visiting Hannibal Lecter in the film *Silence of the Lambs* because I was a woman visiting a dangerous man whom no one had seen or heard of for nearly 50 years. The names of Brady and Hindley are synonymous with child-killers, but the name of Straffen is clouded in a cloak of secrecy.

I handed my VO to the officer. I was told to leave my handbag in a locker; I was not allowed to take in even the simplest of things, such as a pen and paper. The only money I was allowed was a handful of loose change for the coffee machine in the visiting hall. An image of my face was digitally printed on to a security badge. My hand was placed on to store the identifying characteristics of my palm and fingers, and then I was asked to remove my jacket which was put through an X-ray machine.

I walked through a metal detector and was ushered into a small side room and bodily searched, top to toe, by a female officer. I was moved on to several more check points, where on each occasion my handprint was checked and double-checked. Eventually, I went through a turnstile similar to one at a football ground, but this was no game, this was for real. For the last time, my hand was checked and I was told to sit at table number 12. The visitor's area resembled a school assembly hall which had a stage built at one end with five officers sitting behind a blue guard rail. At the other end of the hall was the control unit manned by one officer, guarded by at least eight others.

I looked around; across the ceiling were blue wrought-iron girders with swivelling security cameras monitoring every move. The only indication that they were active was a small, red flashing light. For a moment, I gazed at one camera wondering who might be watching me, but quickly I averted my eyes. Lined regimentally across the hall were approximately 40 low tables, all numbered, surrounded by four chairs that had been screwed to the floor, three beige in colour and one brown.

I sat down in the brown seat at table number 12 only to be told by a burly officer that the brown chair was designated for the inmate only, and that under no circumstances was I allowed to touch the prisoner.

I didn't know what to expect as I waited to meet the man who had spent almost half a century behind bars. I wondered how I would greet him. I didn't want to seem over-friendly or too aloof but, on the other hand, I was the first person he had agreed to be interviewed by.

My thoughts were broken by the activity in the control unit, and suddenly officers were on alert indicating Straffen's arrival. A loud electronic buzzer sounded, an iron door opened, an officer nodded to the control unit and warned, 'Cat-A man coming through.'

John Straffen's 6ft 2in stooped frame appeared in the doorway. He was wearing the prison-issue blue-striped shirt, denim jeans and jacket. Gone was the mop of blond hair which gave the killer a respectable look of innocence way back in 1951. Instead, he was completely bald but had hair sprouting from his ears and nose giving him a sinister appearance. He did, indeed, resemble Hannibal Lecter. I stood up, smiled and, with an outstretched hand, said, 'Pleased to meet you, John.'

His cold, bony hand gripped mine. His eyes gazed unblinkingly. A shiver went down my spine. He sat down in the brown chair and seemed shy and awkward. I asked if he was OK, sat beside him and looked into his haggard face; it was etched with pain, or was it sadness? His eyes struck me first, his piercing blue eyes, like the innocent eyes of a child trapped inside an old man.

I studied him carefully as he began to speak. He whispered politely in a West Country accent that he would like a drink and a piece of cherry cake – if I didn't mind.

I went to the WRVS canteen and returned with four wrapped Genoa cherry cake slices and two plastic cups of tea. I started chatting to him about this book, when he suddenly interrupted me. 'No wipes,' he said. He meant napkins. He wanted napkins. It was almost as though he wanted normality. I went to the counter and found some. I continued to tell him about the book. Again, he interrupted. 'I can't open my cake,' he said as he handed me the small wrap.

He was like a child. An innocent child, one who couldn't even manage the plastic of a piece of cherry cake. Looking at John Straffen, it was almost impossible to believe that, for no rhyme or reason, he had killed three children. He had had no motive for the crimes, none whatsoever, and certainly no sexual motive. There was one word that had been nagging away at me – why?

This was the first interview John Straffen had given and, as his story started to unfold, I thought about the little girls who were still in pig-tails when they tragically lost their lives. Those precious children never experienced any life at all, they never grew into teenagers, or were able to marry and have children of their own, and I felt saddened. But I had to take a step back and suppress my gut instinct to condemn him. I just listened to what he had to say. Whether I liked him or not wasn't important; I wasn't there to judge him, he had already been judged way back in 1951. This is what John Straffen told me...

★   ★   ★

I didn't understand why the judge put the black cloth on his head, he just looked funny. He said they were going to hang me. I heard what the judge said but I didn't understand what he meant.

My mum started to cry, and shouted out in the court that I didn't do it. But they didn't listen; instead a policeman took her away. I wanted to see her to tell her not to cry, but they wouldn't let me.

I was taken to Wandsworth Prison in London and put on E Wing. There were only three cells on that wing, they were known as the 'death-watch cells', like the death-watch beetle, I suppose. These were the only cells in the prison to have two doors, one to enter and one to leave by. If you left by that door you never came back as it led directly to the gallows.

I was on 24-hour suicide watch. That was silly; I didn't need to kill myself, they were going to do it for me. The cell was painted battleship grey and was freezing cold, with a bed, a table and two chairs. I was guarded by six officers on a rota, morning, noon and night; they never left my side for a moment, not even when I went to the toilet. I would sit on the bed all day watching the officers play cards. None of them spoke to me, except one officer, Mr Honey. He would bring me in little treats now and then and sometimes have a friendly word for me.

At night, I used to hear them testing the trap on the gallows to make sure it worked OK. I suppose that's the reason they weighed me to make sure the sandbags were accurate for a clean execution. I wasn't scared, I just went to sleep.

When they told me they had changed their mind about hanging me, I was moved from the death-watch cells to another prison. On one hand I was glad because I would be able to see my mum, but on the other I wasn't, because I was put into the mainstream prison where the other prisoners used to hit me. In the early days, I was beaten up on a daily basis; never a month went past when I didn't have a black eye or a fat lip.

I don't get hit quite so much nowadays. At first, everybody knew who I was and wanted to hurt me, but I've seen so many people come and go, now nobody knows who I am, I've just been forgotten.

The last time I saw my mum was in the late Seventies. She had come to visit me in Parkhurst Prison on the Isle of Wight. The long journey from Bath to Parkhurst proved too much for my mum, she started saying peculiar things on the visit, things I didn't understand. I think she was going mad. The screws had to take her out of the visiting hall; I never saw her again. She died in March 1982. I wasn't told until 12 days later; by then she had already been buried.

I wish I had seen my mum just once more before she died, to tell her I loved her, and that I was sorry. I would have liked to attend my mum's funeral, but it was too late. My brother Roy and sister Jean used to visit me but they stopped. I'm not sure of the reason why, but I can't blame them really.

I spend most of my time locked in my cell. I can't get used to the new central heating system, it's too hot, I've got no control over it, I can't even open a window. The heating system is the only way to judge whether it's hot or cold outside. You see, when you are in prison there are no seasons, it doesn't matter if it's winter or summer, raining or snowing, or even if it's day or night. Your cell becomes your world and the only escape is reading. I like detective books, they're my favourite, but two months ago I thought I was going blind. I was a bit scared, but I had a cataract operation and now I can read better, and no longer need my glasses.

At the moment, my only contact with the outside world are paid prison visitors, but next month I will get my own television set in my cell, then I will be able to watch the wildlife programmes and the cartoons I like — in peace.

Every year I'm automatically considered for parole, but every year I'm turned down. Since 1951, the authorities have used three excuses, which are: I am a danger to the public; a danger to women; and a danger to children. This year, I was turned down for parole without seeing anyone, no interview, nothing. The excuse given — a danger to children. It's just not fair.

I admit I killed the two little girls in 1951 but I said at the time, and I will say it again now, that I did not kill the little girl who was found in Farley Woods. I have no reason to lie, and have nothing to gain.

I think it's time I was released. Although I'm 68 years old, I could still get a job in a factory near the prison. I could tie up bundles of books maybe and earn £5 a week. I'd like that.

There are lots of things I would like to have done but have never been able to. I have never driven a car, or been in an airplane. Never had a girlfriend, never paddled in the sea, stood in the rain or under the stars.

I don't think I am a danger to anyone any more. I'm an old man now. I'm glad they didn't hang me in 1951 but I do believe in capital punishment. Some crimes warrant a life for a life. There are some bad men around nowadays, like paedophiles and sex maniacs; hang 'em, that's what I say, or lock 'em up and throw away the key.

Daniel
Reece

Killers

D anny Reece was accused, and found guilty, of murder. He's now serving life in Whitemoor Prison, Cambridgeshire.

He's also been accused of being a grass. He pleads guilty — with mitigating circumstances. You, the reader, will act as the jury and decide.

On a tape he sent to me, he tried to put the record straight once and for all. He states that he was on a prison landing when a 60-year-old lifer called Ronnie Easterbrook hissed, 'So you're the grass?'

It takes a brave man to stand toe to toe with Danny Reece; all the cons feared Danny. Everyone was aware when he was on the landing. Nobody approached him, or had eye contact with him, let alone insult him by calling him a grass.

So when Ronnie Easterbrook arrived and made his accusation, everyone noticed how he didn't move out of the way or avert his eyes. Ronnie had obviously heard about Danny. His sheer size and strength made him unmistakable.

'So you're the grass?'

A breathless hush swept across the landing.

Danny later told me, 'I felt my blood boil; the palms of my hands began to sweat. I looked into the face of a 60-year-old man who dared to call me a grass. A fucking grass. Being called a grass is the worst insult anyone can give you.

'Everyone on the landing expected me to go berserk, but I didn't — I decided to tell Ronnie Easterbrook the truth like I'm telling you. The man involved was a murdering rapist called Dave Lashley.

'Yeah, I suppose you could call me a grass if you count taking a dirty, rotten, filthy nonce off the streets for the rest of his natural life. The way I saw it was that it could have been my mother, sister or daughter that he'd raped and murdered. I felt I had to do something.

'At the time, I was in Brixton Prison in South London. I was given a job in the wood mill and was allowed to train in the gym twice a week. It was there that I met Dave Lashley, a huge black man who was as strong as an ox. We worked together, trained together and had a laugh. I didn't know what Dave was in for and I didn't ask — it's not the done thing.

'It was just another Tuesday morning and a screw had loaned me a copy of the Sun. The headline screamed out:

black rapist jailed for ten years.

'Dave read the headline. "Ten years," he scoffed. "He should have killed the bitch, he wouldn't have got any more time."

'I couldn't believe what I was hearing.

'"The fucking rapist," he went on. "I killed my bitches. He raped one and got the same as me. The mug."

'For once, I was speechless. This man was a rapist, a murdering, fucking rapist and I'd been knocking about with him. Before I could say anything, Dave grabbed my head, his huge hands holding my skull.

'"This is how I done the bitches," and he began to demonstrate how he'd killed them by pushing his fist into my windpipe.

That's when I snapped. I hit him so hard it lifted him off the ground. As he flew backwards, the screws pushed the panic button, but it was too late, I was on top of him. I really lost it.

'By the time they pulled me off him, both of us were covered in blood. They assumed the blood was mine until they discovered a big piece of black flesh still in my mouth.

'I testified against him in St Alban's Crown Court and the rapist received a natural life sentence. So yeah, I grassed — on a rapist.

'Unfortunately, in prison, things are exaggerated and every time the story is told it gets bigger and bigger. I've even been accused of grassing on Linda Calvey — the woman I love, my own wife!

'What I've said here is the truth. I've put the record

straight. Believe it, if you want to; if you don't, then fuck ya ...'

This is what Danny told me about his experiences ...

★ ★ ★

I've lived in East London for most of my life. I was born within the sound of Bow Bells in Mile End, Bow, which makes me a Cockney.

All I ever wanted was to be like my Uncle George. He was my boyhood hero. I never knew my dad when I was growing up — he gave my mum seven kids then fucked off. I'm the eldest of the seven — I have three sisters and three brothers. Mum did her best for us but quite often we only just had enough to eat.

We lived in an old pre-fab in Manor Road, Stratford. 'The Round House' we called it — it was just like a dome with two bedrooms at the back, a small kitchen, a sitting room-cum-diner in the front and an outside toilet. There was no electricity or gas so Mum cooked on an open fire.

Bringing up seven children obviously took its toll on Mum and she fell seriously ill. This was the early Fifties. Social Services were called in and they wanted to put us into care but Mum's sisters stepped in and the family, us kids, were split up.

I went off to live with Aunt Maud and Uncle George in Leytonstone in East London. I loved it from the start. George took me everywhere with him. He owned a scrap yard and I used to watch him throw car engines across the yard like they were cardboard boxes. I used to search cars for lost money which I kept.

George always had time for me and I wanted to be strong and respected just like him. Maud became like a second mum to me and I loved them both.

When Mum recovered from her illness, we had to go back to the pre-fab. I didn't want to go — I dreaded it. I had experienced living in a proper house with gas and electricity; going back to that poxy pre-fab was the last thing I wanted to do. I had to take drastic action.

Things are simple when you're young — in my mind, if the pre-fab wasn't there, then the problem would be solved … if we didn't have the pre-fab, the Council would have to rehouse us in a proper house just like Uncle George and Auntie Maud. So I went berserk, smashed the windows, ripped doors off hinges, smashed down walls. I totally destroyed the pre-fab. I wasn't caught. My plan worked. The Council were forced to rehouse us.

Not surprisingly, my first court appearance, when I was young, was for criminal damage — I was caught smashing up the toilets in Stratford Station.

Then there was Approved School, then Detention Centre, then prison. Crime goes in steps. You could liken it to an apprenticeship. It starts with small-time thieving, then it progresses to bigger jobs, then the big time, with the odd bit of malicious damage and grievous bodily harm thrown in for good measure until you reach the ultimate goal — armed robberies and murder.

I've been a criminal all my life. I've spent over 20 years in jail for armed robbery and violence. At the moment, I'm serving life for murder.

Was prison a deterrent for me? No. Nothing would have stopped me from a life of crime — it was what I wanted. And prison's too good for some — child-killers should be put down the same as rabid dogs.

Prison used to be a simple place. You served your time, deprived of your freedom, living to rules and regulations that dominated your every hour. But prison today is a far cry from simple. It is full of drugs and people connected with drugs, people who live by drugs and for drugs. The drug tests are a complete waste of time and money; they achieve nothing but have created a prison system which is supposedly there to correct but, in reality, it corrupts.

Heroin is expensive and very addictive. Consequently, the young kids are constantly in debt and are forced into prostitution to pay for their habit. I wish people would understand the stupidity of drugs. The only way out of any situation is to face up to it, confront it, acknowledge it — and change it.

What really gets to me in here are petty people — and people that don't keep their promises. In prison, you meet the very worst sort of human being imaginable and bullies are ten-a-penny. I despise bullies; all bullies are cowards and hide behind the fear they instil in others. But confront a bully and he usually turns into a coward.

I've been stabbed five times — never been shot — but no human being frightens me. I suppose love frightens me the most.

I remember watching my sons being born, and feeling so much for them, and then the saddest moment of my life when my son John died — it was complete hell.

Apart from my sons and my sister's daughter, Tania, I've loved Jennifer, my lovely wife Linda and a little Gremlin.

My future is with Linda; every day and every night I think of her and I write to her every day. I am able to speak to her every fortnight and, if I'm lucky, I get an hour but sometimes it is only for ten minutes. In my dreams, I see myself lying on some exotic beach with my dream girl, counting my millions — or maybe playing in the fields of heaven with my son John.

I suppose the only regrets I've got are not being there to pick up my son from school, and not meeting Ronnie Easterbrook 20 years ago — what fun we would have had! He's the only man I've given 100 per cent respect to.

James
Dowsett

Killers

Everyone in the Suffolk village of Mildenhall mourned when 40-year-old insurance man Chris Nugent was shot to death by a mystery raider as he sat working in his office shortly before Christmas 1987. No one seemed more upset than Chris's business partner and best friend, Jim Dowsett. He attended the funeral and the message on his wreath read: 'Treasured memories of a great man. Twenty years of friendship never to be forgotten'.

To Chris's widow, Linda, the mother of three children, Jim was their closest family friend. Now he was someone strong and supportive to lean on and his shoulder was there for her to cry on. As she wept at the graveside, Jim is supposed to have told her: 'I wish I'd been able to shake his hand one last time. I shall never be able to go to the cemetery again.'

Jim was even at Linda's side when she appeared at a police press conference to appeal for help in catching her husband's killer. Later, she told a newspaper: 'He sat at the same table as me and said that Chris was a kind and gentle man and he couldn't think of anybody who wanted to hurt him.'

A month later, 30-year-old Stephen Gray gave himself up to the police and admitted that he had committed the murder. He said that he and local hardman, 27-year-old Gary Runham, had been paid £20,000 by Dowsett to carry out a Mafia-style hit on Chris Nugent.

Apparently, Jim was due to gain from some life insurance on Chris Nugent, although he told the court that he had only hired Gray to put his partner out of action, not to kill him. However, Gray, who pleaded guilty to murder, told the jury that there was never any question of simply injuring Chris Nugent.

Gray alleged: 'He [Dowsett] said he didn't want them picking bits of lead out of Nugent in hospital and telling him he was a lucky man. He didn't want to look after a cripple for the rest of his life.'

He also said that Jim had instructed him to be careful not to hit the tropical fish tanks in the office because the fish were 'his pride and joy'.

After Jim was found guilty and sentenced to life, Linda Nugent said: 'I hope he rots in hell – he has destroyed my life.' She said that Chris had gone to his death still believing that Jim was his friend and added: 'It's kind of ironic that the trial ended at Easter because Dowsett was a Judas who betrayed his best friend.'

Christopher Nugent's grave is at Lakenheath Cemetery and the inscription the family have put on the headstone reads: 'Stolen from our lives but forever in our hearts'.

Jim is now serving his sentence in Whitmoor high-security prison in March, Cambridgeshire. I sat down among the mainstream prisoners and waited for Jim. I had a rough idea of what he looked like from his newspaper photos but when he arrived he looked older than I expected. He was only 48 but, he said, that's what prison does to you. His sandy hair was thinning and he was shorter and stockier than I imagined. He was wearing jeans and a sweatshirt and he carried a large, efficient-looking folder bulging with papers. I got him some tea and chocolate biscuits and he began to talk. I asked him how he felt when he was sentenced to life.

'I said to myself that I'd never let them beat me,' he said.

I've heard that often enough before – many of the prisoners I've spoken to have said that – but all prisoners cope in different ways. Jim's way was constantly to do battle with what he sees as 'the system'. He chatted on and laughingly told me about a fellow prisoner who sued the prison authorities – and all over a slice of roast beef.

On Sundays the prisoners are served Sunday lunch. However, when this man queued up to collect his plate of roast beef and Yorkshire pud, they told him that they'd run out of beef and he'd have to make do with a slice of corned beef instead. That wasn't good enough, said the man. 'I'm entitled to my slice of roast beef.'

He sued, won his case and was awarded £30 compensation by the courts. Because he was a Category A prisoner, the cost of transport and guards to and from the court must have set the prison authorities back a good 30 grand. A good result, said Jim.

'I won't let them beat me,' he insisted. 'A lot of people inside do it with violence but you can't beat them like that and I'm no fighter. The only way I know how to beat them is through the legal channels. That's how I fight them and I'm like a dog with an old bone. I won't let go. I fight for my rights and the rights of other prisoners. That's what keeps me going.'

I visited Jim at Whitmoor four times. He did show some remorse for his crime but then he also kept insisting that he'd never wanted Nugent killed, just 'bust up a bit'.

'What do you mean?' I said.

'Well, a broken leg – or arm – just so he couldn't work . . .'

You can judge for yourself. In all, Jim talked to me for hours. And this is the story he told me . . .

★ ★ ★

On impulse, I rang Runham that November and arranged a meet. We sat in my car near his house. It was cold, bloody cold. I lit a cigarette, turned the heater up full blast to fight off the freezing weather conditions outside and I told him what I was thinking.

'No problem,' he said, 'but it'll cost you ten thousand.'

'Ten thousand! I think that's a bit steep.'

'Well, you tell me the extent of what you want and I'll give you a price.'

So I told him. I wanted him to bust Nugent up a bit – broken arm and broken leg. I just didn't want him back at work for a while.

'Do it in January,' I said. 'Then I can get the new man into the office to replace him.'

Runham thought about it. 'Seven and a half grand,' he said.

'OK.'

'Five hundred up front, seven thousand after it's done.'

'Agreed.'

He got out of the car and I watched him pull his collar up, put his head down against the chill wind and walk back towards his house. I was excited and nervous. On the one hand my problem was solved – but what a way to solve it. I drove home to Elaine, my wife. I don't think that at that stage it had really sunk in what I had done. The meeting had lasted ten minutes – ten minutes. That's all it took.

I'm not sure when I first got the idea to get Nugent out of the way for a while. It just dawned on me after Runham had come into our office looking for some dodgy motor insurance.

Nugent and I had been friends for 20 years. It was way back in 1966 and a late afternoon when I first bumped into him in the bookies. I had clocked him there a few times before. An ordinary-looking bloke, the man from the Pru (he was working for the Prudential Insurance Company at the time), we were only on nodding terms with each other. Then one day we struck up a slightly longer conversation and from then on we always seemed to meet up and talk in the bookies.

We began to go for the odd drink together and soon we had become what you might call mates. On many occasions I would straighten him out with a few quid as Chris did like a bet and often found himself short. Then he went through a particularly bad patch when he thought his wife was having an affair and, as I was by that time a close friend, he confided in me. 'It's this Green Shield Stamp salesman, Jim,' he said. 'I know it. I'm sure of it.'

I was sorry for him. It sounded like a joke but one look at his face and you could see he didn't think it was very funny, his wife running around with a Green Shield Stamp man. He asked me to help him follow her and I agreed. So I'd drive while we followed her about and he'd peer out of the window, taking photos, trying to gather proof that she was seeing this other man. Chris eventually confronted her with his 'evidence' but it didn't do him any good. She decided to run off with this chap and that was that. It was sad really. But I tried to cheer him up and he often used to come around to our house. The three of us spent many evenings together.

It wasn't long before he started dating a friend of my wife's, called Linda. Now Linda was OK but I always felt that she didn't like me. It wasn't something that I could put my finger on. I suppose the feeling was mutual. Her incessant talking used to drive me mad. There was just something. Maybe the chemistry didn't mix, I don't know, but that didn't matter. Chris was my friend so I didn't have many dealings with her anyway.

When Linda and Chris moved into their first home together in 1976, I used to go round and do the odd job for him. Chris wasn't much of a handyman so I fitted a new bathroom for them and put in all the central heating. I didn't mind. I liked DIY. I helped him in other ways too, like when he tried to get some furniture on HP. He was refused because he hadn't kept up the payments on a new freezer, so I loaned him £500 to help out. I figured that is what friends are for.

They say that you should never do business with friends and, with hindsight, they're right. In late 1986 I decided to take Chris on as a partner and that was the undoing of our friendship.

I thrived on work. I suppose I was a workaholic – Chris turned out to be just the opposite. I wanted to expand my businesses which covered many areas of the financial world. We acted as insurance brokers for various companies, providing life and general insurance and mortgage brokering, and we served as land agents, estate agents, business transfer agents. You name it and my firm did it. All right, not all the work was strictly legit, we had a few fiddles going, but most of it was and it was hard work but I enjoyed it.

KILLERS

In the insurance business you can't always see people during the day so you have to meet in the evenings and I was rarely home before midnight. Chris, on the other hand, was a strictly nine-to-five man and it was beginning to get me down. When he first joined me I did explain that he'd need to work long hours but obviously it didn't sink in. To make matters worse, he began an affair with a girl locally and was always slipping off for a quick leg-over, knowing that I would cover for him in the office. And when he wasn't getting his leg over, he was in the bookies. In the end I was doing his job as well as my own. Chris was fast becoming a passenger.

I thought I'd found a solution when I opened a second branch of the business. Chris could take sole responsibility for that. He would have to pull his weight then and he wouldn't be able to keep sneaking off because, apart from a couple of secretaries, he'd be the only one there.

But Chris would have none of it. He realised that the move would put a stop to his leg-over afternoons and, besides, the new office was closer to his home – and Linda. No doubt he was worried that she'd be able to keep a closer eye on him. So that was that. Chris was determined to stay at the Mildenhall branch. Meanwhile, I was working myself into the ground.

Things were coming to a head. It's funny the things you remember. There was one Saturday in the late summer in 1987. I was sitting there in the office as usual and was feeling rough, run down and full of a terrible cold. I was working on auto-pilot. Chris swanned in.

'You look like death,' he said, 'You shouldn't be in the office.'

I looked at him and waited for him to offer to stay in the office while I went home to bed, but not a bit of it. 'I'd offer to stay,' he said. 'But I've got to take Linda shopping then I'm seeing my girlfriend.'

Looking back, that's when my attitude to Chris really changed. I thought, 'I'm not going to be made a fool of any more.' I started to look for a new partner and I found a man who was perfect for the job, the best in the business. We had a meet and we agreed that he would start work in January 1988. That left me with one problem. What to do about Chris?

Then, in November 1987, quite by chance, a man called Gary Runham came into my office. I'd met him briefly before when he was looking for a mortgage but I didn't know him well. This time he was looking for a cover note for his 3-litre Capri, but he couldn't afford to pay for the insurance in full and, as a favour, he asked if I could let him have the cover note on HP.

He loved his car, he was smitten with it and he kept urging me to go outside and look at it. I followed him outside and was walking around this Capri making all the right admiring noises, when Runham said he used to do a bit of debt collecting when he was in London. 'I had to break a bone or two when they wouldn't pay up,' he said. 'Happened often.' He said that since I'd done him a favour, he'd do one for me. If, at any time, I had problems, he would be only too pleased to sort them out for me.

I didn't pay much attention. I just grunted and went back into my office to get on with my mountain of work. As soon as I sat down at the desk the phone rang and it was Chris — just to let me know that, yet again, he wouldn't be coming into work.

I was furious and in that moment it clicked. Maybe Runham was the answer. Maybe Runham could put Chris out of action for a few months, just long enough for me to rearrange the business and settle in the new partner.

I'd just put the receiver down and the phone seemed to be staring at me. I picked it up again and called Runham. We arranged a meet outside his house in Hertfordshire for the next day. As I drove there I wasn't sure if I was doing the right thing. In fact, I wasn't sure what I was doing. But, I told myself, there was no harm in talking to Runham.

So there we sat in the car on that freezing November day and we settled the price. Runham was cool. I remember thinking how cool he was. Then he wanted some practical details. I told him where Chris lived and suggested he might be able to jump him while he was getting out of his car at his garage at home. There wasn't much lighting there. I told him I wanted the job done in January because that was when the new man could start at the office. Later, he said I'd said I would pay him more if it was done before Christmas. That's not true. I don't know what made him say that. About a week later, Runham phoned. 'I've cased the garage. It's no good. There's no set time for him coming and going. We'll have to think of something else.'

He also told me not to worry if I didn't hear from him

for a week or two. He'd been nicked on a minor drug offence while he had been watching the garage and that meant he had to keep a low profile for a while.

'OK,' I said. 'I'll wait to hear from you.'

I didn't hear anything for a couple of weeks and by that time I was thinking that I had been ripped off for £500. I decided to ring Runham and find out what was going on. His girlfriend answered the phone and told me that Runham had beaten her up and taken off but there was someone else there with her who wanted to talk to me.

When the man came on the phone he introduced himself as Stephen Gray, a name that was to change my life forever.

'Don't hang up,' he said. 'I know the score. I sussed out the garage for Runham. Look, you can trust me. We need a meet.'

I wasn't sure. All my instincts told me that too many people were getting involved but I agreed to meet at a local hotel. I gave a description of myself: 'I'll be wearing . . .'.

The Rutlands is a large, well-established Victorian hotel on the outskirts of Newmarket. It's a comforting, cosy sort of English hotel but I felt uneasy as I walked about the foyer trying to look inconspicuous while waiting for Stephen Gray to arrive. I was nervous and I kept thinking, 'What the hell am I doing here?'

I was just about to turn on my heel and head for the door when in walked Stephen Gray. I knew it was him straightaway. Our eyes met instantly and then he motioned his head towards the door. I went outside and walked to my car. He followed without saying a word.

We sat together in the car and once again he told me that the garage was out of the question and asked me for more details on Chris. What time did he get to the office? When did he leave? I told him that Chris was a member of the local darts team and, as regular as clockwork, he'd walk home alone from the pub on darts night. I figured this would be the best time to catch him.

I also told him that Chris's daughter worked in the office sometimes so to steer clear then. She wasn't in the office on Tuesdays because she was on a training course that day. Gray wanted another £500 up front. I was a bit reluctant to give it to him for the simple reason that if nothing happened then I'd been stung for a thousand in all.

'I'm not ripping anyone off,' he said. 'I mean business.'

So I gave him the £500. He told me that if I saw him around my office I was to ignore him and not to worry, he was only sussing out the gaff. If he had to ring me for any reason, he'd use a code name: Bob Nesbit. God only knows where he plucked that name from. The whole thing was getting out of control and more like some daft kind of gangster movie by the minute.

The next day, 15 December, just ten days before Christmas, I was busy working in the office as usual when the phone rang and it was Gray. 'We're here. Look out of your window and you'll see us. We're parked in the car park of the swimming pool opposite. We're in the orange Princess.'

I said nothing but I was a bit stunned and could feel my heart starting to beat a bit faster. An orange Princess. That was very subtle, for Christ's sake! But he'd told me to ignore them so that's what I did.

I just glanced out of the window. I couldn't see anything, so I carried on working. Later I had an important meeting with an American client at a branch on the other side of town, so I told Chris I was off to meet him and that I would see him later to tell him how the meeting went.

As I got into my car, I could see the orange Princess still parked up. I could just about make out that someone was sitting in the driver's seat. I couldn't tell who it was but I could see more than one person in the car. I was a bit worried and uncertain as I left to see the American client but it was the middle of the day and broad daylight. I felt pretty sure that something was about to happen but not yet, not in broad daylight and not in the middle of the day. So I put it out of my mind and carried on with my business.

The American didn't turn up for his appointment so I was getting on with a mountain of paperwork when, suddenly, the phone rang. Gary, our young office boy, came rushing into the room, his face literally as white as a sheet. 'There has been a robbery at the Mildenhall branch.'

I was stunned, but the first thought that came into my mind was: 'Oh no, they have done it. They've really done it.'

To be honest, I felt sick. I wondered what state Chris was in. I wondered what people would think. Would they guess that I had anything to do with it? I wasn't sure what to do because my mind was racing but I knew I had to get back there, so I jumped into my car and nervously made my way back to the other office.

There were police swarming everywhere, the whole area was cordoned off, and a traffic warden and police officer stopped me from going any further. They wanted to know my business and I told them where my office was. 'What's happened?'

'There's been a robbery. A man has been shot.'

Shot, Christ! I didn't really want to ask, but I did. 'Who's been shot?'

'Mr Christopher Nugent.'

'That's my partner. There must have been a mistake.'

'There's no mistake. I'm very sorry. Mr Nugent is dead.'

Dead! Christ! No! He couldn't be! Jesus Christ what had I done? This was all wrong. He couldn't be dead. Oh my God! The policeman could see my obvious distress and took me to a nearby police car. I couldn't believe it. Why did they kill him? That's not what I wanted. It was all a terrible mistake.

The police drove me home but Elaine was out, Christmas shopping. I just stood in the middle of our lounge and my mind was spinning. I was churning things over and over in my head. I had to talk to Gray and find out what the fuck happened, what had gone wrong.

At around the same time Elaine was walking past Rumbelows when she saw a newsflash on all those TVs in the window. Man shot dead in armed raid! She recognised the office and rushed home.

She didn't know anything. I was panicking. I had to get a grip on myself. I couldn't tell anyone, even her, what I had done. I had to speak to Gray. I must have stood in that front

room for ages. I was frozen to the spot. It seemed like a
lifetime. I was completely unaware of the comings and
goings around me.

There were people phoning to see if I was the one
who'd been hurt and when Elaine arrived she, too, thought
first of all that I'd been the one who'd been shot. It was a
bit like having an 'out of body experience'. It wasn't real at
all. It was as if I was watching all these people running
around frantically answering the phone and making cups of
tea and I wasn't part of it at all. Except, of course, I knew I
was the cause of the whole thing.

A policeman said I had to go to the station to make a
statement. That brought me back to my senses with a jolt. I
knew I had to be careful what I said. I couldn't risk giving
anything away. My mind was in a total panic. At the police
station they took me into a small, cold interview room.
They made me feel like their main suspect from the word
go. That was obvious. In their manner, they were overly
polite to me. They questioned me for hours and I knew
they were trying to trip me up. It was hard to keep calm.

At last, at about nine o'clock, they said I could go. Elaine
had been waiting all this time in the reception. She stood up
and greeted me with a hug. 'What the hell's going on? Why
have they been questioning you for so long?'

I shook my head. 'I don't know, I don't know.' I hugged her
back. I had to keep up the pretence and deny all knowledge.

We came out of the police station and went straight
round to Linda's. A WPC opened the door and, when I saw
Linda come out of the kitchen, for a few seconds I was

worried she'd see the guilt in my face. I was relieved when she threw her arms around me.

We hugged each other and then sat down to a cup of tea. I felt physically sick with guilt and I wondered what she was going to say. I was more than shocked when her first words were: 'Jim, will I be able to keep the house and the car?' Her beloved Fiat! Well, that was Linda.

I looked over to Elaine and frowned but then I assured Linda that I'd take care of everything. I left the house not worried about her problems, only about my own. How the fuck was I going to get out of this mess?

The next two weeks, over Christmas, were a nightmare. I never stopped wondering and worrying about the police enquiries and I had Linda on my back. She was worried whether Chris's insurance covered him adequately. Once again, I assured her that I had everything in hand. I knew Chris was well insured because he had recently renewed his policies. I had taken care of that for him.

There was nothing devious about it as people later tried to suggest in court. Chris's policies were up for renewal but he had gone on holiday and the forms from Crusader Insurance Company arrived for him to sign after he'd left so, automatically, I signed them for him. It's common practice for partners to do and no big deal.

At my trial the police tried to insinuate that this was part of my dastardly plot as this all took place nine months before Chris's death. To be honest, Chris was pleased when he arrived home from his holiday to find that I had taken care of the policy and not let the insurance lapse.

But now Linda was worried that Chris's first wife would end up with a big cut of the money. This came out one night when Elaine and I were giving Linda a lift home. She suddenly asked us to pull into a lay-by. She wanted to talk to us and she didn't want anyone to hear what she was going to say.

She began by asking me if I could arrange things so that she could get all the money. I told her she would get the bulk of it and their children wouldn't want for anything, but she still wasn't happy that her two daughters from her first marriage wouldn't get a share. She wanted it all and suggested that maybe I could fiddle it for her. At the time I thought, 'You money-grabbing bitch.' However, I agreed to do what I could anyway. I still felt very guilty over what had happened.

All this time, I had to keep ducking and diving, being ultra-careful about who I spoke to and what I spoke about. They had closed down the office where Chris had been shot as they were searching for evidence.

I was scared stiff that they'd go through our paperwork and find out about our dodgy mortgage deals. Superintendent Abrahams was in charge of the case. Everywhere I went, he was always turning up, asking me questions, trying to trip me up, and all this time I hadn't heard from Gray and I had no way of contacting him.

I was terrified that someone would find out that I was the one who'd wanted him hurt, that I was the one who had set Gray on him. I felt it was my fault what had happened. Whichever way you looked at it, it was all down to me.

Before he died, Chris had left some Christmas presents with me and he'd told me that his son wanted a remote-control car. So now I went out and bought the boy a good one. Elaine rewrapped all the presents – she had to because one of them was for Chris's girlfriend but we weren't sure which one and we didn't want Linda to find out about her.

On Christmas afternoon we took the presents round to Linda's. It was awful sitting with the family watching them open their presents. Linda had become very clingy to me. She seemed to rely on me. I was taking care of all the bills. Her stepfather asked me to take care of the funeral expenses – I agreed. It was the least I could do. I was also giving her £100 per week. I wanted to help her in any way I could, to ease my own conscience I suppose.

That Christmas afternoon was really hard to swallow. I was smiling, saying the right things, but behind the veneer I was a tortured man. Straight after Christmas there was to be a press conference. Linda wanted me to take her. 'Come with me, Jim,' she said. 'I need support, I can't do it on my own.'

I could hardly refuse but little did she know that, Jesus Christ, I needed support too. I was dying at the thought of so many millions of people watching my every move. I can't tell you how pleased I was when it was all over. I couldn't get out of that police station quick enough. Not only were the public watching me on television, but I could also feel Superintendent Abrahams's eyes burning into me.

At the end of December the police pulled me in again, this time to make a formal statement. They were still being overly nice but all the time they would slip in slight suggestions about what they thought had happened and what they'd heard. This made me very uncomfortable. And still not a word from Gray.

On the second of January the call finally came. Elaine picked it up and a gruff voice said, 'I want to talk to Jim.'

She asked who was speaking.

'Bob.'

'Jim, it's Bob on the phone!' she called. She obviously thought it was another Bob, a man who owed me some money. I did too – I'd forgotten his code name was to be Bob Nesbit but as soon as I heard his voice I knew it was Gray.

'It's me,' he said, 'I need money. Meet me at the same hotel as before. Tomorrow, twelve-thirty. Be there!'

My heart was suddenly in my mouth. I couldn't say anything or ask anything because Elaine was only yards away, so I just said: 'Yeah.'

The next day was Sunday. I knew I had to meet Gray but I did not relish the thought. I didn't know what was in Gray's mind and the urgency in his voice worried me. So, for moral support more than anything, I asked a good friend to come along with me. I didn't give him any details, I just told him that I had a meeting with someone a bit dodgy and that he needn't get involved. 'Just wait for me in the car for half an hour,' I said. 'If I'm not back after that time, call the Old Bill.' That was all he knew and, being a good friend, he didn't ask any questions.

I saw Gray walk past the hotel. I got out of my car and followed him as he walked slowly to a secluded car park at the back of the building. It was very dark and there was no one around. He looked desperate, all unshaven and wearing a long, dirty trench mac. As I approached, his eyes scanned around, watching every move I made and beyond me to see if anyone else was about. The only sound was the rustling of the trees. As I got closer, I blurted out: 'What the fuck happened?'

'The shooting was an accident,' he said.

'For fuck's sake! Why? What happened?'

'I had to do it then. There's people I owe in London. I had to give them the money.'

Then he told me what had happened and it was a bloody cock-up from start to finish. Gray said he'd gone into the office by the side entrance and found that Chris was alone. He asked him about the possibility of arranging a mortgage in the hopes that Chris would invite him behind the counter. But he didn't and, while they were talking, someone banged on the back door. It was a salesman but, instead of telling him he was busy, Chris invited the salesman in, told him he had a client in the front office and asked him to wait out the back as he wouldn't be long.

The salesman sat down in the back office with a cup of coffee. Chris closed the door and went back to Gray. Things were starting to go wrong and now Gray was beginning to panic. The sawn-off shotgun he was carrying fell out of his inside coat pocket. Seeing the gun, Chris dived under the counter. Gray told me he thought Chris was going for a gun, so he shot him, the first barrel unloading straight through his neck.

Gray then jumped over the counter, pointed the gun at Chris's head and shot him again at point-blank range, full in the face. Some fucking accident! Chris was unrecognisable. Gray stepped over the body and rummaged around to find the money which I'd told him I kept in a filing cabinet. Amazingly, through all this the salesman stayed out the back drinking his coffee. He later told the police that he thought the two loud bangs were fluorescent light tubes exploding!

I couldn't believe what Gray was telling me. It was so cold blooded, his words seemed to freeze as he was saying them. I couldn't move. I just stood there listening. Then his mood changed – very nasty.

He said, 'I want money. The nine grand I got from your office has all gone.'

'But I haven't got any more – just a few hundred.'

'That's not enough,' he snapped. 'I want grands – five at least.'

'I just don't have it.' I said.

He was angry and growled, 'You get me the fucking money or else! I've already killed once and I'll do it again, only this time it will be you or one of your family.'

I felt sick. I knew he meant it so I tried to stall him. 'I need some time.'

'You've got a week,' he said. 'Come Friday, if I don't have the five grand, I'm coming looking for you. Next time I see you it'll be to put a bullet in you.'

I had to think quick so I gave him the phone number of a friend of mine and told him to phone the number in a week. He said, 'I'll phone it on Thursday and it had better be sorted.'

When I got back home I phoned the friend, who was called Roger. I made up a story about a customer who wanted a loan of £5,000. I told Roger that I couldn't get the money myself because of all the trouble with Chris being shot but if he could get it for me I could guarantee to pay it back personally at the end of the month, with a good drink on top for himself.

Roger said that would be no problem. Christ, what a relief! I told him that the customer would phone and then come and collect the money himself. He'd say only that I had sent him. That's just what Gray did and that, I hoped, was that but I was being foolishly optimistic.

Two weeks later, Roger phoned me. He was not at all happy. He said that the man who had collected the five grand was back and now he was in his office demanding a further seven grand. 'What's going on, Jim?' Roger asked. 'What's this all about?'

What could I say? I could hear Gray in the background shouting, 'Tell him to give me the fucking money or he knows what will happen. He'll get what the other fella got.'

I said to Roger: 'Look, I'm in deep trouble. I can't explain. Please could you help me?'

Roger is a good friend. He said he could loan me £3,000 but that was all he had and, after that, he wanted nothing else to do with it. I couldn't blame him. I heard him tell Gray that he could only give him three grand and Gray went mad. I could hear him shouting: 'I want more or I'll give you both barrels, same as Nugent!' He wanted the money and he wanted it now. Roger said they'd have to get it from his bank in Swaffham in Norfolk.

Meanwhile, I had to scrape up as much as I could. I arranged to meet up with Gray in a pub called the Swan in Hillbrough. Gray wouldn't let Roger out of his sight for a minute and followed him into a nearby public toilet. Nervously, Roger handed over the envelope containing the crisp new notes and told Gray that he didn't know what was going on and he didn't want to know. He gave Gray directions to the Swan but Gray didn't know the area and he was becoming agitated. 'You're going too. You're going to take me there.' Roger had no choice and reluctantly drove him to the Swan where I was waiting.

I'd been at my wits' end trying to pull up more money. I went around all my friends and gave them some cock and bull story. In all, I managed to raise a further £4,500. As I drove to the Swan that cold January lunchtime my mind was in a complete turmoil. The lounge bar was empty. I walked up to the bar and ordered a half of lager. 'Anything to eat, luv?' the barmaid chirped.

I was so nervous that I knew if I ate anything it would have stuck in my throat but I wanted to look and act as normal as possible, so I ordered some scampi and chips in a basket. I paid for the food and went to the gents to gather my composure. I could feel the beads of sweat on my forehead starting to trickle down my face. I had to get a grip on myself. I had to act normal. I had to look right. I ran the cold tap in the wash basin and cupped my hands.

The ice-cold water felt good on my face and, just for a moment, I wondered if I was going mad and this was merely a nightmare.

When I walked back into the lounge, my food was on the table and at that moment Roger walked in, looking anxious. Gray was behind him. 'Take it outside, Jim,' Roger said. 'Leave me out of it.'

I walked out to the car park with Gray following me. I saw a new Honda parked alongside mine. The engine was running and a girl sat in the passenger seat looking around nervously. Gray tapped me on the shoulder. 'Got the money?' I turned towards him and gave him the cash, then he said he'd be needing more.

'I'm going to buy a hamburger stall on the South Coast,' he said.

I snapped. 'For fuck's sake, I've got no more. I've not got an endless pit of money.'

Gray screamed back. 'You'd better find it or I'll do you and all your family. It's Monday now – you've got until Thursday.'

I knew he meant what he said. As he walked past me he poked a finger in my face, narrowed his eyes and in a quiet voice he said, 'Thursday, 8 p.m., the service station on the M25. Don't be a silly boy. Don't let me down.' He then got in the car and drove away.

I went back to the office. I didn't have a clue where I was going to get the money from. As I walked in, I noticed the light was flashing on my answerphone. I slumped down at my desk and pressed play. Shit. I couldn't believe it. I recognised the voice immediately. It was Runham, the man I'd first approached to hurt Chris.

'I need money,' the message said. 'Meet me Friday and bring two grand with you.' I couldn't believe what I was hearing. Now this bastard was trying it on too.

I spent the next couple of days trying to get some more money together for Gray. He was a madman. God knows what he'd do if I didn't give him some more. I got together all my credit cards and cleaned them out and then I called in a few outstanding loans. All in all, I managed to scrape together a further £4,500.

That Thursday night it was pouring with rain. I walked into the service station bang on 8 p.m. and ordered a cup of coffee. I sat at a table in the corner and I must have stirred my coffee a hundred times. Gray walked in. I got up from the table and went into the gents. I met him there and gave him the money. 'Look, that's every penny I have. And now Runham wants money. He wants a meet tomorrow.'

'Don't go,' said Gray. 'It could be a set-up. I'll be in touch.'

Yeah, for more fucking money, I thought and watched him hurry out.

I decided not to go on the meet with Runham. I had nothing to give him. I just stayed in my office, scared stiff to answer the phone. By this time I really didn't know which way to turn.

However, things were happening that I didn't know or hear about until later. All this time Gray and his girlfriend had, apparently, been staying at a bed and breakfast place in

Newmarket. That weekend Gray had an argument with the girl and she went back to her sister's in Wales. The pressure had started to get to her so, when she got home, she told her sister the whole story about Gray and the shooting. Her sister persuaded her to go to the police and, before long, they'd put out a newsflash with Gray's picture and a description of his car. After that it was all over.

The landlady at the B and B recognised Gray and phoned the police. He sussed something was wrong and had it away on his toes but he must have known the game was up. On 25 January 1988 he phoned the police and agreed to give himself up – in the company of his solicitor.

For a week he kept quiet. Then, after a tip-off, the police arrested Runham. He'd been bragging about his involvement with Chris's shooting in some pub.

All week I kept hearing stories that two men had been arrested for Chris's murder but I still didn't know who they'd got. Then the police came and formally told me that they'd arrested two men – one called Gray, the other Runham. As the police officer told me their names, my skin went so tight it felt like it had shrunk.

I knew now it was only a matter of time before they pulled me in. The week that followed was terrible. There were so many rumours flying around and every time there was a knock on the door, or the phone rang, my heart felt as if it had stopped. Also, Superintendent Abrahams, was, it seemed, stuck to my hip. I couldn't move. Whenever I looked out of the window I could see an unmarked police car. I knew that wherever I went they were following me.

Whenever I made a phone call I would hear a click as I lifted up the receiver. Abrahams made no secret of the fact that he suspected me.

That week I tried to prepare myself for the worst. I had been arrested before so I put 40 fags, two boxes of safety matches and a notepad and pencil in my jacket pocket, just in case. I tried to put Linda's affairs in order and my own. By then it was obvious that it was only a matter of time.

After a week of interrogation Gray finally cracked and spurted out the whole story. He admitted killing Chris, but said it was all down to me, that I had paid him 15 grand with a five grand bonus if he did it before Christmas. Why he said that I still don't know. And then there was all that stuff about me saying: 'And don't shoot the fish.' That was nonsense. I never mentioned the bloody fish.

It was six o'clock on the morning of 1 February 1988 when the police finally arrived and arrested both me and Elaine. It was pandemonium. I was in my striped pyjamas, the police were shouting, our five dogs were barking and the house was full of blue uniforms. We were both handcuffed and charged with 'conspiring to kill Christopher Nugent'.

It had finally come on top. My only thoughts now were to inform the police that Elaine was an innocent party in this whole fucking mess. Later, I'm pleased to say, they dropped all charges against her. With me, on the other hand, it was a different matter. Eventually, the police charged me with the murder of Christopher Nugent and I was jailed for life.

So were Gray and Runham but Gray, the man who pulled the trigger, became eligible for parole in 1996. I am not eligible for parole until 2005. It feels a long time away and I wish to Christ I'd never got involved with them.

As far as Chris is concerned, I very much regret what happened, of course I do. I wish now I'd just fired the bugger.

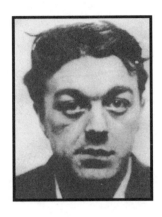

Harry
Roberts

Killers

In 1966, Harry Roberts was Britain's most wanted man. On Friday, 12 August, in a quiet street near London's Shepherd's Bush, he and two accomplices gunned down three policemen in cold blood.

Until then, the murder of a British policeman was virtually unheard of. To most people it was the kind of thing you only saw in Hollywood gangster movies. The crime, and the front-page photographs of three bloodied policemen lying dead in the street, shocked the country. The British public was outraged.

Two of the killers – John Duddy and Jack Witney – were arrested within a week but it was three long months before the police caught up with Harry Roberts who was hiding out in a barn in the Hertfordshire countryside.

During those weeks, the police mounted the biggest manhunt the country had ever seen. Everyone was looking for Harry Maurice Roberts. His face, with large staring eyes, looked out from the newspapers and television screens almost every day. He was armed and dangerous, they said, and he shouldn't be approached.

Policemen from all over turned up at Shepherd's Bush police station during their off-duty hours, offering to help, and messages came from every chief constable in the land offering assistance from his force 'no matter how menial the task.'

The police received thousands of calls from the public – 10,000 within a few days. All reported 'sightings' of the fugitive. He was spotted rowing across to the Isle of Wight in an open-topped boat; he was seen in St James's Park in London; in Germany, the police arrested a man called Roberts and held him for three days before he managed to persuade them of his innocence.

All the sightings were false alarms but every one was followed up. At different times, various London houses were surrounded in the middle of the night, swooped upon by hundreds of armed policemen and searched. One day, after a tip-off, dozens of men from the police special patrol group searched the famous Sadler's Wells opera house during a rehearsal of Offenbach's opera *Bluebeard*. (Tenor Emile Belcourt, dressed for his part in a black riding costume and cloak, sang on, supported by a male chorus of five and a pianist. Later he said, 'In this profession you don't falter even if the place falls down around your ears.')

Harry was reported to be hiding out in a girls' school in Dagenham; he was seen walking into Harrods wearing a pin-striped suit; he was spotted on a BEA flight to Birmingham and in a house in St Ives in Cornwall; and dozens of strippers ran screaming and half-naked from the stages of several Soho clubs after a series of police raids.

Sixteen thousand wanted posters were printed and displayed outside police stations throughout the country. They offered a reward of £1,000, which was a fortune in those days, but nothing worked. Harry Roberts, it seemed, had disappeared.

What shocked people particularly was the brutality of the crime and the apparent lack of motive.

It was high summer and it had been a pretty routine day for the three plain-clothes officers who made up the crew of the unmarked 'Q' car patrol, Foxtrot Eleven – called the 'Q' car after the 'Q' ships of the First World War, which tracked down U-boats while disguised as innocent merchant ships.

In command of the three-man crew was 30-year-old Detective Sergeant Christopher Head who'd recently been promoted. His second-in-command was 26-year-old Detective David Wombwell, the father of two children. The third officer was Constable Geoffrey Fox, a local man and father of four.

The officers were on the nine to five shift and had just enjoyed lunch in the Beaumont Arms, close to Shepherd's Bush police station. They were on their way to Marylebone Magistrates Court when they were passed by a blue-grey van, registration number PGT 726, carrying three men.

The van was in very bad condition, it didn't display a tax disc and was making a lot of noise. The officers were suspicious and they decided to stop it. While Officer Fox remained in the patrol car, Officers Wombwell and Head approached the car. Within minutes all three had been shot dead.

Several people witnessed the shooting, including some young children who had been playing nearby. One man, who had seen the van reversing at high speed down a street, had made a note of its number because he thought there might have been a break-out from Wormwood Scrubs which was just up the road.

Thanks to his quick thinking, the van was immediately traced to Jack Witney and within 24 hours he had been pulled in by the police and was being questioned at Shepherd's Bush police station which now housed the murder incident room. He claimed that he'd sold the van that same day to a man in a pub for £150. No one believed him – a little boy who had seen Witney in the van with Harry and Duddy had given an excellent description of him. The boy was a football fan and he told the police that one of the men was the spitting image of his hero Bobby Charlton – Witney looked uncannily like the World Cup star.

The police soon found the van in a lock-up garage south of the Thames and inside it they discovered some spent .38 cartridges and the remnants of a pair of stockings, of the kind robbers often used to hide their faces during hold-ups.

Witney was charged with murder and, not wanting to take the rap alone, he soon grassed on Harry and Duddy. Duddy was picked up in Scotland and, under questioning, both he and Witney claimed that it was Harry who had instructed them to shoot.

Four days after the killings, the police issued their first description of Harry. He was 30, they said, five feet ten inches tall with a fresh complexion, brown hair, blue eyes with a half-inch scar below the left eye and another less obvious one at the base of his thumb. When last seen he had been wearing a grey suit, white shirt, dark tie and brown suede boots.

Very soon they gave out another description. They had been tipped off that a man looking suspiciously like Harry had bought outdoor clothing and camping equipment from a shop in King's Cross. Now they urged the public to look for a man wearing a checked shirt, a khaki combat jacket and trousers and grey boots and carrying a grey rucksack.

Three hundred policemen, many carrying rifles and others with dogs, descended on Epping Forest and carried out an inch by inch search. Armed detectives also flew over the area in five light aircraft.

They were on the right track but they were too late. As Harry explained to me, he'd already left Epping Forest and was on his way to Thorley Woods, near Bishop's Stortford. That's where he was finally picked up 12 weeks later.

A policeman stumbled across his camouflaged tent, on the edge of woodland close to a disused airfield and within a few hundred yards of a gypsy camp. Detectives couldn't believe how neat and tidy they found everything in Harry's hideout.

His clothes had been kept scrupulously clean and so had

his pots and pans. He'd made a kind of cabinet from cardboard and plywood and in it he had stored tins of food and trays of fresh eggs. Clean tea towels were stacked close to his two sleeping bags. He also had a brightly coloured collapsible armchair in one corner of the tent, a new foldaway camp bed and, to keep his food warm when he was out hunting, a metal hotplate which he'd made from the base of an oil drum.

Harry's army training had served him well and he obviously hadn't forgotten army discipline. As one reporter wrote, 'Even the Wellington boots, used for tramping through the woodland, were clean.' The makeshift camp was described as 'cosy' and 'ingenious'.

Knowing the police were on his trail Harry had already made his escape but he was soon found in a barn nearby. He was handcuffed, taken to Bishop's Stortford police station and given hot tea and a meal of minced-meat pie and vegetables from the police canteen. He was then charged with murder and he's been in custody every since.

I first met Harry in Gartree High Security Prison in the late eighties. By then he had served over 20 years. It was a brief meeting. I was in Gartree visiting my brother-in-law Reggie and he introduced us. Later, when I told Reggie I was writing this book, he offered to contact Harry who'd since been moved to Nottingham.

Within a few days, Harry was on the phone to me. 'Don't talk on the phone,' he said, 'it's all taped. Do you want to visit?'

I said I'd love to see him. 'When can I come up?'

'Well,' said Harry, 'I'm here most days!'

He sent a VO (visiting order) and a letter (he has the most beautiful handwriting) and I travelled up to Nottingham. It's an old prison and a bit bleak, but the visitors' hall was OK, with ladies from the Women's Institute serving up tea in the corner.

Harry was waiting for me, looking fit and well and dressed in the usual prison 'uniform' of sweatshirt, jeans and trainers. We got on well from the start. He's a very interesting man and he obviously likes to be the boss. I have quite a strong personality and, in most of my interviews, I was the one asking the questions and directing the conversation but with Harry it was different. He took the lead automatically. Our first meeting was spent discussing this book. Until he knew exactly what I was aiming to do, Harry wasn't prepared to talk about his own life. Afterwards, when he started talking about those days in 1966 when he was on the run, he made it clear that he wanted to tell it in his own way. 'Write this down,' he'd say. I'd started to write notes but he would have none of that.

'No,' he said. 'No notes. You must write down exactly what I say.'

Harry has recently become a member of Mensa and I soon ended up calling him the Mensaman. He was very patient with me when I couldn't follow what he was saying. At one point he mentioned the word 'coppice'.

'A coppice? What's that?' I said. 'How do you spell that? Do you mean a bush?'

'No,' said Harry, 'I mean a coppice,' and he quoted as if

from a dictionary: 'A wood of small trees, cut periodically.'

'Who are you? Mensaman?' I said. Harry roared with laughter.

I wanted the story of what really happened on the day those three policemen were shot and I wanted to know about his life during the three months he was on the run but Harry had other stories to tell too.

He was born in Wanstead in Essex in 1936. His father and mother worked at The George in Wanstead. His parents got divorced when he was five and that was more or less the last he saw of his father. He was an only child and probably the most important woman in his life was his mum, Dorothy, who died in the 1980s, a couple of years after Ron's mum, Violet, passed on.

I'd love to have met Dorothy Roberts – she sounds like a very sparky lady. Harry was the apple of her eye and she worked hard to make sure he never went without and to put him through college. She never deserted him. For the first ten years of Harry's imprisonment she was the only person who was allowed to visit him and she was always trying to get him out – by hook or by crook! When Harry was first in Parkhurst Prison, on the Isle of Wight, visitors were allowed to bring in food for the inmates and Harry roared with laughter as he described how his mum would bring him strawberries and fairy cakes.

'I'd be sitting there and I'd go to take one of the strawberries and she'd whisper, "Don't take that one – it's got a compass in it!" or I'd take a fairy cake and she'd say, "No, not that one! There's a file in there."'

In 1973 she was charged with and later acquitted of helping Harry to escape. She'd smuggled some bolt cutters into the prison in her bra!

She went to the toilet and hid them under a floor polisher for Harry to pick up later. However, the screws became suspicious when they saw Harry eyeing the hiding place!

Harry told me that he was amazed when he read the reports in the newspapers about his mum's court case. 'It said she was seventy-four,' he said. 'I didn't have any idea how old she was and I told her so when she came to see me – "I didn't know you were seventy-four, Mum!" I said. "Well, how old did you bloody think I was, boy?" she said.'

All in all, in the time Harry has been inside, he tried to escape – and failed – 22 times. The year before his mum brought in the bolt cutters, one of his most audacious plots was foiled. Somehow he'd managed to get hold of a masonry drill, a metal bar and a pair of pliers and he was attempting to tunnel through his cell wall, which was three feet thick.

When the screws finally swooped, they also found sunglasses, a compass, wire-cutters, a knife, a gas lighter, maps of the Isle of Wight and four five pound notes.

Harry had been confident about that plan. He'd gone to a lot of trouble to persuade the prison officers that he was really quite happy and settled in Parkhurst! He'd spent hours digging a goldfish pond among the prison's vegetable plots and was seen to take great pride in looking after it. After he was rumbled, however, the authorities quickly moved him on to Leicester Prison. Just as with Reggie, they didn't like the idea of Harry getting too settled in one place and would move him on regularly before he got to feel too 'at home'.

However, moving Harry didn't stop him from planning more escapes. Another of his plots was even more daring. He was in Leicester Prison at the time and he'd become friendly with an IRA man. Together, they hatched a plan: they'd build a crossbow and fire an arrow, with a line attached to it, across the prison walls into a nearby park. IRA men, who would be waiting there, would attach explosives to the rope and Harry and his accomplice would haul the explosives back into the prison. Then they'd blast their way out. They made the crossbow successfully but realised that they had no elastic to power it. A relative of the Irishman came up with the solution — she knitted Harry and his friends lots of tank-top jumpers which she sent as presents to the prison. The bottom rows of the jumpers were knitted with strong elastic which could be unpicked!

Maybe it would have worked but they never got to find out. Harry drew a plan of the prison and a map showing the park and where the crossbow's arrow was to land. He hid it in the back of a painting that he was sending out of the prison. As the picture was going through the security system, his home-made frame broke and out fell the plan. That was the end of that.

At one time Harry was also in trouble with the prison authorities for suspected drug dealing but that was a long time ago and he has never been involved in drug dealing. He hasn't attempted to escape lately either. Now, he tells me, he is definitely going straight.

All the time I was with him he was cheerful, charming and friendly but, beneath that, I have often wondered what kind of man he really is. You only have to read the stories about his life until he was 30 to know that he was ruthless.

He freely admits that this triple life sentence isn't his first conviction for violent crime. In March 1959, he appeared at the Old Bailey charged with robbery with violence. He and an accomplice had broken into an old man's home posing as income tax inspectors. They had smashed a glass decanter over his head, tied him up and rifled through his belongings looking for money and valuables. Harry was shopped by his wife, picked up by the Flying Squad and arrested. In sentencing him to seven years, Mr Justice Maude said, 'Harry Maurice Roberts, you are a brutal vicious thug. You came very near the rope this time. It is to be hoped you do not appear before us again.'

In fact, the old man died one year and three days after the attack – just two days outside the time limit for murder.

Violence always seems to have been part of Harry's life in the early days. Perhaps that's why he did so well in the army. Unlike Ron and my brother-in-law Reggie (who've always said they were 'temperamentally unsuited' to army life), Harry loved it. He was called up for National Service in 1956, after he left Borstal, and, as Rifleman Roberts, army number 23275696, was posted to Kenya and Malaya. A tough, restless man, the life of a soldier suited him and he was promoted to sergeant. When he was demobbed in 1958, he left with a 'good character' but he soon turned to crime. Maybe he was bored, maybe he needed a challenge, maybe he should have stayed in the army.

His only marriage was a disaster, but he was obviously very much in love with Lilly Perry – the former wife of a Bristol policeman – with whom he was living at the time of the Shepherd's Bush murders. Like his mum, she was loyal and loving.

He told me: 'It's bad after the visitors have gone. They bang us up at five for a couple of hours while they have their tea and I find myself thinking: "Where's she now. I wonder how many miles down the motorway she is now? Perhaps she's stopping for a cup of tea at a motorway cafe now . . ." It's a form of mental torture.'

One of the things that has kept Harry going while he's been in prison is his painting. Before starting this stretch Harry had never painted but once he got into it it was obvious that he had great talent.

The prison authorities encourage long-term prisoners to paint in the hope that they can form a better understanding of them through their work. Harry dismisses that. One psychologist talked in great detail about one of his paintings, claiming it showed all kinds of emotional turmoil. 'What turmoil?' said Harry. 'I got the idea from a picture on the cover of Marvel comic!'

Harry's paintings are extraordinary – very exact and precisely drawn and coloured – and many of them show someone shooting a policeman.

One of the saddest conversations we had was when he told me that he'd decided to give up painting – at least until he gets out. 'I was painting a landscape,' he said, 'and I came to paint a tree, but couldn't. I couldn't "see" the tree. I couldn't paint the tree. I realised just how many years it had been since I had seen a real tree growing in the wild and I couldn't "see" one in my mind any more.'

As a present, I took him a bonsai tree and he was well pleased but he still says he won't be picking up a brush again. He now suffers from arthritis in his fingers and glaucoma which, he fears, is slowly making him blind.

As well as painting, Harry also used to make jewellery boxes and sell them to earn a little bit of cash. Reggie gave me one once – a jewellery box with a painting of a barge on it. It's beautiful.

His artistic exploits didn't end with paintings. Harry is famous throughout Britain's prisons and one ex-lifer told me that he remembered Harry in one prison as 'the Pastryman'. 'He used to do the most beautiful pies,' he said, 'but, instead of decorating them with pastry leaves and flowers, he'd do a pastry picture of someone shooting a copper!'

I told Harry about this and he said, 'Yes I'm famous for my apple pies . . .'

Of course, what he is most famous for is the crime he committed that summer's day in 1966. Summing up at the end of his trial, Mr Justice Glynn Jones described the murders as: 'perhaps the most heinous crime to have been committed in this country for a generation or more.'

I don't know what remorse Harry feels now for what he

did. I think he believes that, after all this time, he has served his time and deserves a chance.

> Harry Roberts, is our friend,
> Is our friend, is our friend,
> Harry Roberts is our friend,
> He kills coppers!

(A verse that was sung to the tune of 'London Bridge is Falling Down' by London children in the sixties.)

★   ★   ★

Friday 12 August 1966

It was the first day of the shooting season. The glorious twelfth! And it was a glorious day too – hot and sunny.

Me and Lilly were staying with a friend of ours in Maida Vale, called June. She was a right tart and the place wasn't much but she had two lovely kids. I had a cup of tea and a piece of toast and then left the flat at 8.30 a.m.

Me and two mates – Jack Whitney and John Duddy – were planning a robbery at the local engineering works and we needed cars. We'd decided on three for the job and they had to be good. High performance. Two Jags and a Ford Executive would be ideal. So we got into Jack's van and went looking for them. We drove to Regent's Park and cruised around the outer circle. We normally went down there to nick our cars because we knew the commuters parked there all day while they were working and it was common knowledge that no one would notice the missing cars until about 5 p.m. By that time we were long gone and, nine times out of ten, we would have done the robbery.

We spotted the two Jags we needed but couldn't find the Ford Executive and the day was wasting away. We ended up driving to Harrow and found a Ford Executive parked down a sidestreet next to the tube station.

Me and Jack got out of the van and sneaked across the road to nick it. Jack crouched down, pushed a small piece of wire in the lock and jiggled it up and down and then, much to my annoyance, he broke the 'jiggler'. I got the right hump and stormed back to the van. It was all a waste of time. Jack jumped in the driver's seat and we drove off to Northolt to look at the engineering factory.

We drove around for a while and I was getting right pissed off. The morning had gone and we had not done a thing. So we decided to go to the pub and have some lunch. After a pint and a game of darts, we thought we'd better go back to work.

We were driving down Erckwald Street when we spotted a Triumph 2000 following us. There were three men in the car. I turned to Jack. 'That's the Old Bill. I bet they're going to nick us.' He looked worried and carried on driving. We drove into Braybrook Street. It was 2.45 p.m.

The car overtook us and stopped about 130 feet ahead. One of the men got out of the car and started to come towards the van. We were panicking trying to hide all our tools including the shooters. The man, who turned out to be PC Wombwell, came around to Jack's side of the van and

Jack wound down the window.

'I'd like to see your driving licence and insurance certificate,' he snapped.

Jack reached into the glove compartment and gave them to him. Wombwell walked back to the police car and we could see him talking to the other officer, Sergeant Head.

Jack handed me the 9mm Luger that he had under the dashboard. PC Wombwell returned to Jack's side of the van. Now he wanted to see what was in the back. 'Fuck off,' said Jack and a violent row erupted. Sergeant Head came around to my side of the van and, with my elbow, I quickly flicked the switch down so he couldn't open my door. That annoyed him and he started shaking the van, grabbing hold of the door handle and screaming, 'Open the fucking door!' Me and Jack looked at each other. By this time PC Wombwell had his head through the open window, screaming at Jack.

With half a smile, Jack said quietly, 'Let the slag have it, Harry.'

Instantly, I raised my arm and, with the Luger Jack had just handed me, I shot Wombwell point blank. The bullet whizzed past Jack's nose and hit Wombwell just below the eye. He slumped to the ground. I could hear my heart thumping. The air was electric.

I turned towards Sergeant Head. My elbow caught the door knob and the door flew open while he was still pulling on it. I could see the shock and disbelief in his eyes. I jumped out of the car still holding the gun. Sergeant Head turned and started running back towards the police car.

I aimed my gun and fired. I got him right in the middle

of his back. He went down like a sack of shit. I ran up to him. He was lashing out with his legs. I held his legs, aimed my gun at his head and pulled the trigger. Click. It was a dud. I took a step back and ejected the blank from the chamber. Then I tried to grab his legs again but he kicked me in the face, making my nose bleed and splitting my lip.

Again, I aimed the gun at his head but, to my horror, it was another dud. I couldn't fucking believe it. He was struggling like fuck and managed to get to his feet and he started to run again. But he only made it to the front of the police car and fell in front of it.

At that moment there seemed to be a slight lull. I heard Jack shout, 'Get the driver!' I looked towards the van and saw John Duddy standing in the road like some kind of cowboy. He was holding his gun out in front of him and 'fanning' the trigger. I hadn't noticed the police car starting up. PC Fox, the third man in the car, had been sitting there, watching. Now he crunched the car into reverse gear. Suddenly Duddy shot all the windows out and there was glass flying everywhere. PC Fox was in total panic and rammed the gear lever into first in a vain attempt to get away. But as the car shot forward he ran over Sergeant Head who was lying in front of the police car, wedging him under the back wheels. At that moment I turned to face the driver, only to see him take a bullet in the head from Duddy. I saw him slump down over the steering wheel. It was as if he just went to sleep. In less than 30 seconds all three police officers were dead.

Jack had already jumped out of the van and taken all his papers from PC Wombwell's body and was now back in the driver's seat with Duddy in the back. The van had started and was beginning to move. I ran towards it and, for a moment, I thought that they were going without me. I shouted, 'Wait for me, you bastards!' and I dived into the passenger's seat, and screamed, 'Go! Go! Go!'

We screeched backwards out of Braybrook Street. Jack was driving like a madman. We drove backwards all the way down Erckwald Street and we were reversing down a third street when we cut across a geezer in a Ford. He took down the number of the van. Jack spun the van around and we drove away at top speed into Oak Lane. At that moment a police motorbike came alongside us. Jack said, 'Give it to him as well' but the copper must have realised he was in danger because he quickly veered off and I lost sight of him.

We carried on across Hammersmith Bridge, continuing down the South Bank side of the river towards Vauxhall. As we approached Battersea Bridge roundabout, I couldn't believe it when the van started to pink and slow down!

'What the fuck's happening, Jack?'

He slapped the steering wheel in frustration and said, 'Jesus Christ! We're out of petrol!" He kept his finger on the starter motor button and, like a kangaroo, we jumped down the hill to where we could see a garage.

We pulled in behind a Triumph Vitesse. An old lady in a tweed suit was sitting at the wheel. There was only one attendant and, just our luck, the old dear had decided to have the works: 'Can you check my oil?' she said. 'What about the water?' It seemed to take forever. We were all trying to act normal.

In the distance, we could hear the sound of the police bells ringing. Duddy yelled at Jack to hurry up. But the old dear wasn't going to be rushed. We had to stay calm. At last we got some petrol and sped off to the lock-up garage in Timworth Street where Duddy and I got out. The lock-up was by the railway arch and Jack crunched the wing as he pulled into the garage.

He then joined me and Duddy down on the Embankment.

'What the fuck we going to do?' said Duddy.

'We got to get some dough,' said Jack.

I thought there was only one thing we could do. 'We will have to do a bank.'

'No way,' said Duddy, and with that he went, 'Fuck this, I'm off'' and he ran off down the street.

I watched him disappear down the road and I looked at Jack. The sweat was pissing out of him. He was scared. All he wanted to do was go home. So we jumped on a number 68 bus to Euston. By the time we reached Euston station, less than an hour and a half after the shooting, there was already a news billboard reading: 'ONE DEAD, TWO INJURED'.

We went into the station cafe and had a cup of tea.

'It's no good,' said Jack. 'We'll have to kill the other two.' I agreed and we caught a cab back to Duddy's to let him know what we had in mind. As the cab pulled up I went into the newsagent's on the corner of the road just as the newspapers were being delivered off the van. I noticed the front page as the man slung them across the pavement. It read: 'THREE DEAD'. I walked into the paper shop just in time to hear someone say, 'I bet I know who did that.' I looked around quickly but they weren't talking about me, thank God.

Duddy's flat was on the eighth floor and he always used to look out of his toilet window to see who was approaching. As he saw me and Jack walking up the path, he leaned out of the toilet window and shouted, 'Thank fuck, it's all three!'

We sat talking about what we were going to do and thought it was a good idea to split up. So Jack went home and I went back home to Lilly. As I walked in, Lilly said, 'Have you heard the news? Three policemen are dead!'

'Have I heard it? We fucking did it!'

That night was the longest night of my life. I couldn't eat, I couldn't sleep. Me and Lilly stuck to the telly and were watching the news when the newsreader announced that Jack had been arrested and taken to Harrow Road police station. The van registration number had been traced back to him. Shit! But at least they couldn't find the van.

Saturday 13th

The first thing I thought of in the morning was that we had to get rid of the van. We had to burn it. I went round to Duddy's flat. He said he felt trapped eight floors up so I got him to come round to the flat at Maida Vale. He wouldn't ride in my car so we walked. As we were walking down the Portobello Road, all of a sudden we heard the sound of a police car coming towards us with its bells ringing. I froze but Duddy took off like a shot. I found him in the newsagents, hiding in the corner pretending to read *The Times*. The bells had been nothing more than an ambulance on an emergency call-out.

When we finally got back to the flat, Duddy collapsed on the couch. He was in a terrible mess. He couldn't eat or drink; at any little noise he leapt to his feet. I knew the only thing that could tie us in with the shooting was the van. I had to get rid of it. I had to find a way. As time was going by I was getting more and more paranoid. I couldn't think straight. Duddy was making me uneasy. By the afternoon, I just had to get out of that flat. I suggested that we all go to the park with June's two kids. As we were walking through the park, two police officers were walking towards us.

My heart was in my mouth as they got closer. I said to Duddy, 'I think this is it, I think it's all come on top.' Duddy panicked. He picked up one of June's kids, put him on his shoulders and tore off through the park. I put my arm around Lilly and took a deep breath. As the police officers walked passed us, they both said, 'Afternoon'. I nearly died. We went back to the flat and decided we had better stay put until dark then we had better go and torch that van.

Duddy was no use at all so it was down to me and Lilly. We waited until 10 p.m. Lilly drove a car that she had hired earlier in the day. We drove slowly towards the railway arches. It was really quiet and nobody was around. I didn't like the look of it. I kept thinking it was an ambush. We decided to park the car in the next street. Lilly stood guard at the top of the road.

I tried to keep in the shadows. I squeezed the handle of my gun tight. The only sound I could hear as I got closer to the lock-up was the thumping of my heart. I was scared stiff.

The closer I got to the lock-up, the more I was convinced it was an ambush. I couldn't do it – my bottle went. I turned and hurriedly made my way back to where Lilly was waiting for me. I grabbed her hand and said, 'Let's get the fuck away from here.'

Sunday 14th

Early on Sunday morning we went to bury the guns – a Luger, a Smith and Wesson and a Webley – up at Kenwood on Hampstead Heath. Duddy was still in a right state. He wanted to go to Scotland and promised he would go to Dundee. He thought he'd be safe there. I was becoming increasingly paranoid and Duddy was becoming a burden so I gave him £30 and told him to fuck off.

I knew I couldn't stay at the flat any longer so I packed a bag and arranged to meet Lilly under the clock at Paddington Station at 3 p.m.

It was a lovely sunny day so I decided to kill time in Hyde Park. I wandered around for a while and lay on the grass to do a bit of sunbathing. But I felt as if there was a huge neon sign on my head with a big arrow pointing at me saying, 'Here I am, I'm the murderer.'

I got to Paddington Station to meet Lilly and I stood at the top of the ramp and looked down. I could see her standing under the clock. I was nervous as I made my way towards her. I felt sure everyone was looking at me but they weren't. It was just me being paranoid. I hugged Lilly. It was good to see her. It seemed she was the only friend I had in the world. We decided to stay in a hotel and found a reasonably priced one, called The Russell Hotel, in Russell Square. We went in, trying all the time to act normal but everything seemed to be such a hassle. I asked at reception if they had a room.

'Would sir like that with a bath or a shower?'

'Oh, yeah, whatever.'

'And would that be a double bed or single beds?'

'Oh, yeah, double. Double will be fine.'

By this time I was thinking to myself: 'Just give me the fucking key, you old bastard.' When he eventually did give me the key, the room was on the top floor. I felt trapped. By this time I was getting very jumpy.

I had the idea that I would dye my hair blonde, so I told Lilly to go to the chemist on the corner and get me the dye. 'Get one with peroxide in,' I told her but, much to my annoyance, she came back with a rinse instead. I reared up at her. I was becoming unreasonable in my behaviour. I even pulled the wardrobe in front of the door so no one could get in while I was asleep.

When we went to bed that night, Lilly snuggled up close. It was good to feel her warm body against mine but when she started getting all fruity I said, 'Leave it out Lil.' I couldn't raise a smile, let alone anything else. I don't think I slept a wink that night. I remember just sitting on the bed watching Lilly sleep. I knew it was getting time for me to leave her. It was getting too dangerous to keep her with me. I knew that when the police did finally catch up with me they would probably kill me.

Monday 15th

We booked out of the hotel early. I had it in my mind what I was going to do. I was going to drop Lilly off then go and hide in the woods. First, though, I had to get some supplies so we made our way to Camden Town and bought some camping equipment, a sleeping bag, a small stove, heavy boots, a camouflage jacket and a small radio. Then we got some food: a loaf of bread, three tins of baked beans, Oxo cubes, a packet of tea and some dried milk. I stocked up on Old Holborn tobacco and green papers. I stuffed everything into a large rucksack and we caught a number 720 Greenline bus out of Camden Town to Epping Forest.

We got off the bus at a small country pub called The Wake Arms, which is on the edge of the forest. Lilly was wearing her best coat and high-heeled shoes and she held my hand tight as we made our way deep into the forest. She never spoke a word, not even when she snagged her coat on a bramble.

When we stopped, I changed into my new boots, lacing them up slowly. We both knew the time had come to split up. I turned to Lilly and said, 'It's time I was on my own, Lilly.'

She started to cry and said, 'But I can help you. Please let me stay with you.' I was choked up and tried to explain that it was me they wanted, not her, and I would have a better chance on my own. She had been so good, so loyal and I loved her so much. I couldn't put her life in danger any longer. I promised that I would phone her at a phone box in Maida Vale every Tuesday afternoon at 2 p.m.

As we made our way back to the edge of the forest, she held my hand tight and tried not to let me see her crying. It nearly broke my heart as I waved her goodbye on the bus. I don't think I have ever felt as lonely as I did at that moment.

I got myself together and made my way back into the forest. I pulled my heavy rucksack on my back and started to make my way down the A11 on the edge of the forest. After a while, a car pulled up with four men in it. The driver shouted out: 'Where you going, mate? Want a lift?'

I tried not to look round to let them see my face. 'No thanks,' I said.

'Go on, jump in. You don't want to walk with that heavy pack on your back.'

I thought to myself: 'For Christ's sake just go away,' but they were insisting that I get in. 'No,' I said, 'I don't want a lift.'

'Well, fuck you,' one of the men shouted. 'Hope your feet drop off, you ungrateful bastard!'

So now there I was having an argument with four men in a car when all I wanted to do was blend into the countryside.

I wanted to get out of Epping Forest. I reckoned the police would look for me there. I knew exactly where I was heading – Thorley Woods, near Bishop's Stortford. I knew the woods there like the back of my hand as my mother used to take me there regularly as a kid. And I also knew that the only person in the world who would know where I was was my mum and that was comforting to me.

After walking for about three hours, I turned on my small radio to listen to the six o'clock news. I heard the newscaster say that Duddy had been arrested in Scotland. Two down, one to go. I was determined not to let them catch me. I quickened my pace. My feet were killing me. I had been walking for hours and it was starting to get dark. I had to keep going. By eight o'clock I was fucked. I just couldn't walk any further. I found a coppice of trees and decided to make camp there for the night.

All I wanted to do was get my boots off and have a cup of tea. I hadn't had a drink for hours and was spitting feathers but I didn't have any water. I looked around and came across a cattle trough in a field. I wiped away the green scum on the top, filled my small container with the murky water, took it back to the coppice, boiled it up and made the tea. It tasted like shit but was the best cup of tea I have ever had.

I took off my boots and slowly peeled off my socks, along with most of the skin from my heel. The blisters were three deep. It felt great to have my boots off and I soon fell asleep, totally fucked.

Tuesday 16th

I woke with a start and sat bolt upright. At first I couldn't make out where I was. I thought I was having a bad dream, a nightmare, but then it hit me and I remembered it was no dream, it was real. Every bone in my body ached. I had a wash and a shave in the leftover water from my container. Then I leant against a tree and tried to pull on my boots. The pain from those fucking blisters was unbearable. However, I knew that Thorley Woods were only about another 12 miles away, so I packed up the rest of my stuff and made my way back to the road on the edge of the coppice.

By the time I reached the next village, called Sawbridge-worth, it was lunch time. As I was walking down the narrow street, I passed an old lady working in her garden. 'Morning,' she said. 'What a lovely day! I bet you enjoy your life, don't you?'

I answered her with a grunt. 'Oh yeah,' I thought, 'fucking great if you only knew!'

I knew I wasn't far from Thorley Woods now, so I quickly got on my way. It was dusk by the time I reached the edge of the woods and all I wanted to do was sleep. I thought I would sort out my hideaway the next day.

Wednesday 17th

I woke up early and was freezing cold. My clothes were damp and my feet were hurting like hell.

I gathered up my rucksack and made my way deeper into the woods. I needed to find somewhere completely isolated, where ramblers and dog walkers wouldn't venture. I came to a small clearing that was perfect and started to make a low shelter. I spread my ground sheet out and cut bits of wood about 18 inches high to hold the top sheet up. I had a good look around the area and found some old fertiliser bags that I stuffed with straw to lie on. I was feeling right pleased with myself and thought that no bastard would ever find me.

I unpacked my little stove and made myself a nice cup of tea. After my tea I was feeling brave and decided to make my way back to the edge of the woods and do a bit of sunbathing. I stripped off my shirt and lay down. It was a lovely day. I must have fallen asleep and I was woken suddenly by a man calling to me, 'Afternoon!'

I thought, 'Oh fuck!' and for a split second I was afraid he was a policeman because he had a blue shirt on. He wasn't, but it was enough to put the wind up me. I couldn't take any chances and sneaked back into the woods. The rest of that day I just slept to make the time go quicker.

Thursday 18th

I turned on my radio and heard that there had been a running gun battle at Nine Elms in London. Three friends of mine called Billy Gentry, John McVicar and Ginger Cooper had had a shoot-out with the Old Bill. I was glad. I thought it might take the dairy off me, although I still wasn't one hundred per cent sure that they even knew it was me. My name had never been mentioned in any of the news reports, only that they were hunting a third man in connection with the murders.

Friday 19th

My radio was my only form of communication with the outside world so I only listened to it at newstimes. I didn't want to waste the batteries. Suddenly, I heard a familiar voice on the radio. I thought, 'Fuck me, that's my mum!' I shot up quick. Now it was confirmed that they knew it was me. I knew it was only a matter of time, how long I didn't know.

I listened eagerly to my mum's voice, waiting for any hidden message in her words. My heart was thumping and I turned the radio up full volume but it still didn't seem loud enough. I pressed it close to my ear. Her words were going over and over in my head.

'If you're listening Robin, give yourself up! This is your mum speaking. Don't kill anyone else. Please, Robin, listen to what I'm saying.' (She was the only one who ever called me Robin.) She carried on: 'I'll come with you if you give yourself up. We'll go together. This is your mum speaking. Everything will be all right, Robin.'

My heart sank at the sound of my mum's voice. She sounded so sad and alone. I just wanted to go home and give her a cuddle. I knew she knew where I was but she wouldn't tell those bastards anything. Her voice went off as quickly as it came on. The other news continued. I left the radio on for a bit, hoping to hear her voice again, but after a while I turned it off. Then there was just silence.

I felt that my life had been smashed up. Everyone was against me and I had no friends. I knew now I had to be doubly careful. From that day, I didn't come out of the woods for three weeks, except once to phone Lilly and at night when I would sneak out to get water from a stream two fields away. On Tuesday 23 August I first tried to phone Lilly. I had left the woods and it was getting close to two o'clock and I had to find a phone box to phone Lilly as we had arranged. I dialled the number and I nearly had a fit when a man's voice answered. 'Who's that?' the voice said.

At first I thought that maybe it was just someone using the call box. So I said: 'Is there a girl there called Lilly?'

'Hang on,' the voice said.

I didn't like the sound of it. I was sure it was a set-up and the police were trying to trace the call so I said, 'Bollocks!' and slammed the receiver down. I was worried. What had happened to Lilly.

I had to get myself into some kind of routine. For a start, I had to ration my food. I figured that I had enough to last me for about three weeks if I was careful, so I was only eating every other day. I'd already spent two terms in prison. I didn't want that again. I was still determined that I wasn't going to be caught or give myself up. I was alone now with just my thoughts. I had a lot of time to go back over my life ....

I was first nicked when I was 17 years old, when I walked into a tobacconist and asked the shop keeper for a book that was on the top shelf. When he turned around to get the book down for me I coshed him over the head with an iron bar and stole all the money from the cash register.

I legged it out of the shop and across the road. In those days there were hardly any cars on the road but from out of nowhere a car appeared and chased me around the narrow streets, cornering me at the end of a dead-end alley. A giant of a man unfolded from the car, grabbed me by the scruff of the neck and marched me off to the local nick. By this time I was quite well known by the local police. I was remanded in custody and taken to Wormwood Scrubs. It was my first taste of prison.

I was taken through the reception. As I was being led through the prison to A Wing, I thought that the entrance of A Wing resembled a church. I looked at the screw and said, 'I don't go to church, mate.'

Before the words had hardly left my mouth the screw punched me straight on the side of the head and said, 'I ain't your fucking mate, and this ain't no fucking church.'

I was soon to learn he was right about that. He opened the gate of A Wing and pushed me through.

I will never forget that first experience. It was just like you see in the old black and white films – wrought-iron landings with rows and rows of heavy locked doors. But the thing that struck me most was the silence. The place was completely quiet, like a morgue. All the time I was there I was always in bother, although it wasn't long before I was on the move.

I was transferred to Gaigns Hall, a Borstal in Huntingdonshire, where the regime was really strict, concentrating on work and physical fitness. I did the rest of my time there, 19 months in all. I was eventually released in January 1956.

I was right pleased to get home with my mum but after only seven days of freedom I was called up for National Service. As it turned out, I loved the army. I didn't find it too difficult. On the contrary, after Borstal, I found the army quite easy! So did many of the Borstal boys. We seemed to get on a lot better that the ordinary civilians who were called up. Army life agreed with me. I loved the discipline and it wasn't long before I was promoted to corporal.

I think I must have acquired my fascination for guns while I was serving in Kenya, fighting the Mau Mau. I killed for the first time in Malaya while we were fighting the communist terrorists. It was jungle warfare and there was a curfew in the rubber plantation area between 2 p.m. and 6 p.m. I was on bandit patrol, carrying my FN self-loading rifle.

Then I came across an Indian man. I had him in my sights when someone shouted, 'Rubber thief!' Now, being a thief myself, I just couldn't shoot him. So, instead, I captured him, much to the annoyance of my superiors. I really got in hot water over that and nearly lost one of my stripes.

Afterwards, I was determined that the very next time I saw a bandit, I would shoot him, which I did. Under those circumstances you are never really sure if it's your actual bullet that does the killing or not, but I believe that that was my first experience of killing another human being.

On returning from Malaya, I tried to get into the SAS but ended up in the second Paras in the Territorial Army Regiment at White City. That didn't last long and I was soon back home with my mum in her small flat in Camden Town. I was happy to go back to the bright lights of London's West End and I was eager to get back to grafting. I needed money and I felt strong and confident because now I was always armed.

My life of crime had moved on from simple burglaries to hold-ups, banks, wage rolls, bookies, etc. With this came an increase in violence and soon violence was part of everyday life for me.

Banks were a pushover in those days. All you needed to do was wave your gun around, jump over the counter and help yourself. I was meeting up with old faces and things were starting to come together. Looking back, those days were great and I was always flush with money. At night, and at weekends, I would go to the all-night cafes and pick up a 'mystery'. A 'mystery' is a girl who has run away from home up north or wherever. You could always tell them by their worn-down shoes and we called them 'mysteries' because they were girls with no history.

On one of these nights I met a mystery called Connie. I went out with her a couple of times and she was OK. A few days later I saw her again in the cafe and she introduced me to her friend Margo Rose Crooks. What a name. And what a girl! She was a club girl, standing four feet ten inches tall and the most beautiful girl I have ever seen in my life. From that moment, I fell bang in love with her. We married a month later, at Easter 1958, at St Pancras Town Hall. It was a small wedding and we moved in with my mum. Unfortunately, Mum hated my new wife from the word go and wouldn't even talk to her so it wasn't long before we got a couple of rooms to ourselves in Swiss Cottage.

Life with Margo was one big merry-go-round. She lived life at 100 miles an hour. She was so much more experienced than me. She liked all the good things in life; her only downfall was that she was a pisshead. One of our regular haunts was the new Cabinate Club, in Gerrard Street, which was owned by Jimmy Cooney who was later shot dead by Jimmy Nash, a good friend of mine.

One night me and Margo had been drinking heavily. We had a right row upstairs in the club and I tried to throw her out of the window. She was dangling by her legs, screaming her head off, when Jimmy Cooney stopped me. He then threw me out of the club. That night changed my life. I went home to my mum's. Margo stayed at the club drinking and she was arrested in the early hours of the morning for being drunk and disorderly. The next day she appeared at Bow Street and was fined ten bob, which she didn't have. In those days you were only allowed one phone call and she used hers to ring my mum's while I was at work. She asked Mum for the ten bob, but Mum wasn't having any of it and told her to 'piss off'.

After Mum put the phone down, she came to the building site where I was working to tell me what had happened and in my lunch break I went over to Bow Street to pay her fine. As soon as I went in the nick I knew something was wrong. I said to the desk sergeant, 'I've come to pay Mrs Roberts's fine.'

He said, 'She's gone. Her fine's already been paid. Who are you?'

I said, 'Don't worry who I am.'

I sussed there was something going down and made a hasty getaway straight through the courts.

As the Old Bill didn't know my face in that nick, I went back to work that afternoon, thinking that I would sort it out that night with Margo. While I was working, I saw the Flying Squad come on to the site and go into the foreman's office. It wasn't long before I was face down on the ground. Margo, my beloved wife, had sold me down the river for ten bob.

She had grassed me for a 'tie-up' I had done three months earlier. The house was in Burma Road and me and a mate went on the 'tie-up'. We bashed the bloke about a bit and ransacked the house, not finding anything. The next day in the papers it said the man was on the danger list. We never heard anything else about the man and we thought he had died. So, you can imagine my horror when the police arrested me and threw me in the police van.

They were kicking the shit out of me, saying they were arresting me for the Burma Road 'tie-up'. They took me to Highbury Vale police station. I was scared stiff but I never said a word. I thought I was going to be 'topped'. It was 1958 and hanging had not yet been abolished. It wasn't until the arresting officer said, 'I can't make up my mind whether to charge you with attempted murder or robbery with violence!' and I heard the word 'attempted', that I relaxed. I beathed a deep sigh of relief, I can tell you. I was eventually charged with robbery with violence and was sentenced to seven years.

I have never seen Margo from that day to this. I would have killed her if I had, no doubt she knew that. She sent the police to collect her belongings. The nine-month romance ended with the girl I loved selling me down the river for ten bob.

This time I did four years and eight months out of the seven-year sentence. I told the authorities that I had changed my ways and no longer wanted to live in London and, if they could arrange for me to go to a hostel in somewhere like Wales or Bristol, I would start afresh and go straight. Much to my surprise, they gave me a hostel in Bristol and let me out on early parole.

It was while I was staying at the hostel in Bristol that I met Lilly in a pub called The Victory. I was 27 and she was 40, an ex-policeman's wife. It wasn't long before I moved in with Lilly. She was a wonderful woman, really easy going. Nothing bothered her. I could come and go as much as I liked, she would never ask me any questions.

I was soon back to my old ways, travelling to London in my shiny new black Daimler to do my villainy, then coming home to Lilly in the evening. I would never do any hold-ups in Bristol. I would never shit on my own doorstep. I even started a building company, subcontracting for Wimpeys. I never made any money from it but it was useful as a front.

It was on one of my many jaunts back to London that I met up again with an old pal of mine, a man by the name of Jack Whitney.

I first met Jack in 1958, in a club in Sussex Gardens, Paddington. He was six years older than me and he was a good villain, very well respected. As a youngster, I looked up to him and sometimes he would let me go on tie-ups with him, but only as a driver. I wasn't good enough to go in on the tie-ups.

I had met up again with Jack while doing my seven stretch in Maidstone Prison; he was there doing a three for robbery. Often, when I was visiting London, I would take Lilly with me and she became friends with Jack's wife. We even went out as a foursome sometimes.

Now me and Jack were working together regularly and I loved it. He was a real pro. Jack had another pal he worked with, a man called John Duddy. So, I suppose, you could call us a little firm now and things were really moving for us. Like me, Jack also had a legit business as a cover. He drove a lorry in West London. Having a cover business was essential. Although our hauls from the robberies were never much more than two or three grand, this money had to be accounted for if we were ever unlucky enough to get nicked.

Our robberies were becoming more and more daring. Looking back on it, I suppose we were all heading for trouble but then I'd always been in some kind of trouble or another. I never gave it much thought. I was always thieving and never worried about the consequences. Funnily enough, my mum always called me Robin but my mates said it was because I was a 'Robbing Bastard'.

My mother had me quite late in life and I was an only child. She worked as a barmaid and my dad was the cellarman at The George pub in Wanstead.

At the beginning of the war, they left the pub and bought a café in North London. She worked every hour

God sent to earn enough money to put me through college. I went to St Joseph's College, Norwood, South London. At the age of 14, however, I was expelled and went to a local school for the last year.

For as long as I can remember there has been villainy around me. My old mum's café was a haven for black-market or knocked-off goods. I was the café kid, the one who was always collecting or delivering parcels with no questions asked. In 1951, after leaving school, I had numerous jobs but was finding that burglary was fast becoming my chosen profession. Looking back on it now, I suppose I gave my poor old mum a lot of heartache over the years and I regret that.

I thought about that a lot while I was hiding out in the wood – I didn't have much else to do but after three weeks I had to get myself together and be practical. My rations had all but run out two days before, I had scraped the green mould off my last slice of bread and, since then, I had only eaten ears of corn from a nearby field. I was now very hungry and weak and I knew I had to go out and get some food and supplies. The thought terrified me but I knew I had to go.

By this time I had grown a goatee beard and 'tash, thinking that they changed my appearance. I thought that I would go to the supermarket in the nearby town of Harlow. I made my way to the main road and the bus stop.

The bus seemed to take forever to come, but finally one did arrive. Even with my so-called disguise, I still felt very conspicuous and when the bus reached Harlow I jumped off and went into the first tobacconist that I came to. I couldn't believe it! On the front page of all the newspapers was a picture of me! Just my luck. I had come out of hiding on the very day the three coppers were being buried.

My first reaction was to grab the pile of newspapers and run but I had to keep calm. My hands were shaking as I paid for my tobacco and I couldn't get out of that shop quickly enough. I found the supermarket and quickly got some shopping but my nerve had gone. I'd had enough of being out in the open. I jumped on a moving bus that read Bishop's Stortford. I was more than glad to get back to those woods.

I built a fire, made a big pot of tea and toasted the bread. It was good to eat again and I ate the whole loaf. I felt much better now with food inside me. I didn't like the vulnerable feelings I had had in the town. I had to get my guns because I felt naked without them so the next day I got a Greenline bus to Camden Town, then a bus to Hampstead Heath and walked across to Kenwood.

Me and Duddy had buried the guns in the woods just down from a broken fence stake. When I got there, to my horror, someone had mended the fucking fence so I couldn't find the right spot.

When I eventually found it, I dug them up with my bare hands. I tucked the Luger down my belt and stuffed the Smith and Wesson in a plastic carrier bag. I reburied the Webley revolver just in case I needed it at a later date. I was now armed and felt confident again. As it was Tuesday, I decided that instead of phoning Lilly at two o'clock I would surprise her by meeting her at the phone box.

I was walking along Albert Road, heading for Maida Vale, when I noticed a copper coming towards me. I felt all the muscles in my body tighten. My instinct was to cross over the road but that would have looked suspicious as there wasn't any pavement on that side.

It was no good, I had to front it out. As we passed each other I didn't want to look at him but, then again, I didn't want to look away. My throat was dry and I couldn't swallow. When he had passed, I wanted to look around but I couldn't, just in case he had turned around too. I closed my eyes tight. I thought that any second I was going to feel his hand grab my shoulder. I hurriedly made my way to some nearby public toilets. I was shaking. I couldn't risk another situation like that.

I pinned the right hand sleeve of my jacket up, leaving my arm free inside my coat so that I could keep hold of my gun all the time. I knew which way Lilly would be walking so I started to head that way. I was early as it was only 1.45.

As I turned the corner, I felt that something wasn't right. The road seemed empty. There was a sort of calmness in the air. I looked up and down the road, my eyes scanning for any movement. Then, all of a sudden, I clocked a CID officer sitting in his car, a right bastard called Ginger Hemsley. It was him all right. You could tell him a mile off. He had a mop of ginger hair and always wore brightly coloured bow ties.

I jumped back against the wall and froze. For a moment

I didn't know what to do. I saw him look down at his watch. By now it was nearly two o'clock. He started his car and screeched around the corner to the phone box. I turned the other way and started to walk quickly back up the road, only to pass another police car making its way to the call box. The place was swarming with them, but I kept calm and walked right through them. Something must have gone wrong. Lilly would never have told them about the call box. I was sure of that but how could they have known? I had to talk to her.

I made my way to Leicester Square tube station, where I first bought a ticket to Aldgate. Then I went to a call box and phoned our friend in the upstairs flat. When Andrea answered I said, 'Can I talk to Lilly please, Andrea?'

'You've got to be joking,' she said and put the phone down.

I went straight down the tube, got on the first train that came in and I went to Charing Cross where I changed trains for Aldgate.

When I got to my platform, I saw another policeman waiting there. I just panicked and jumped on the first train I saw moving out of the station. I didn't know if I was being followed but I couldn't take any chances. I stayed on the trains for a while, changing at different stations until I got to Aldgate East where I got off the tube and walked to the Greenline bus depot at Aldgate. When I got there, there was a copper sitting on a motorbike outside the station. My mind was in a turmoil. I did not know what to do. Everywhere I went there was a copper waiting.

I wandered down a backstreet where there were a lot of winos and down-and-outs lying in doorways. I came across a rundown cafe. It was the pits — full of down-and-outs — but I walked in and ordered myself a cup of tea. A filthy slob of a man serving behind the counter handed me a chipped cup of lukewarm slop. The cafe had only one spoon in the whole place and that was chained to the wall. I looked around at the tramps who were in that cafe. I thought I had problems until I saw those poor bastards.

I bounced out of that cafe feeling a lot better and caught a tube back to Tottenham Court Road then on to the Central line to Epping Town. By the time I got off the train it was 10.30 p.m.

I asked a man what time the last bus went to Bishop's Stortford. Just my luck, he was a talker; he kept chatting on and on, asking me all sorts of questions. I told him that I was looking for farm work but he wouldn't let me go. He just kept waffling on. I was so pleased when a Greenline bus came along that I jumped out in front of it and flagged it down. Thank God, I thought, the bus was empty. I went to go upstairs but the conductress said it was downstairs only. I slumped down on the long seat just inside the bus and asked for a ticket to Bishop's Stortford, but it was the last bus and she said it was only going as far as Harlow Town. 'That will do,' I said. I was the only person on the bus and the conductress started to chat.

'Why didn't you thumb a lift?' she said.

'I tried. No one would stop.'

'You know why that is, don't you?'

'No.'

'It's that Harry Roberts. He's still on the loose, you know. Imagine stopping to give someone a lift and you turn round and it's him! Sod that!'

I thought 'Soppy bitch, you just did'.

She carried on, 'Mind you, I could tell him straight away.'

'Oh yeah, how?'

'He has a big scar above his left eye.'

I turned my head and pretended to look out of the window, trying to hide the scar that she would know me so well by. I had a good conversation with her, all about Harry Roberts, and when I finally got off the bus, she called out to me, 'You take care now, he's a bad one, that Harry Roberts.'

What a fucking day. I was glad to get back to the woods.

After that my bottle had gone and I decided not to go out in broad daylight for a while. By day I would sleep but by night I was my own person, free to do as I pleased and there wasn't anybody going to stop me. I had my guns and I felt safe and was prepared to use them if I had to. I started to get my life in some kind of order. I sorted out my food problems. I found a poultry farm and allotments and would nick the odd carrot and tomato out of someone's greenhouse.

I had all the food I wanted. I had a kettle and a tilly lamp and would sit, quite contented, by my fire. Then I noticed that I had started talking to myself. I would say things like, 'Think we need some more wood?'

'Well go and chop some then.'

I started to get a bit worried. This wasn't good. Another problem was money. The cash I'd had with me when I first went on the run was nearly all gone. I had to do a few burglaries to get more. So at night I would go to the town and break into factories looking for money. I broke into a school and got a big box of pennies. I broke into an office and found the keys to the safe. I couldn't believe my luck. There was a few hundred quid in there and that lasted me for a while.

One night, when I was out doing my rounds, I walked past a garden and noticed a rabbit hutch. I sneaked over the fence and started to make my way up the garden path. All of a sudden I heard this thumping noise, as if someone was running downstairs. I jumped behind the dustbin and waited, my heart pounding. Again I started off down the garden path and again I heard the thumping sound so I dived behind the garden shed. Every time I got closer to the rabbit hutch the thumping sound got louder.

I didn't know that when a rabbit senses danger it thumps its back legs. I was really annoyed that this fucking rabbit had kept me in that fucking garden for an hour, so I opened up the hutch, grabbed it by its ears and stuffed it in my sack. Above the hutch was his name: 'Timothy'. I thought, 'I'll give him Timothy!' I took him back to my camp, held him by his ears and said, 'Your number's up, Tim!' Then I shot him in the head, skinned him and made a stew.

Staying put in the woods by day and venturing out by night was doing my head in. At times, I would actually get used to living in the woods and forget why I was there.

When you're cut off from the outside world your mind starts to play tricks on you and I thought that maybe, just maybe, they had forgotten all about me. In a way this was quite dangerous. It gave me a false sense of security and on these days I would go out in daylight. I would often go to Kentish Town baths and have a good old scrub. I also went to the pictures.

There was one freezing cold day when I went to Warner Brothers, Leicester Square and saw the war film Battle of the Bulge. I came in halfway through the film and I remember feeling very relaxed and totally absorbed in the picture. When it came around to the part where I'd come in, I stood up to leave and out of the darkness a hand reached out and touched me on the shoulder. A man's voice said, 'Oi!' I thought it was the police.

I quickly spun around with my gun in my hand but the man was just trying to watch the film and I was in his way. We stared at each other for a few seconds. I left in a hurry.

I was always having problems with my guns. Whenever I was out they were forever dropping on the ground or slipping through my waist band and down my trouser leg. So I bought myself some strips of leather to make two gun holsters.

They weren't much better. One was so fucking tight I had trouble pulling the gun out, and the other one was so loose that when I bent over it fell out. As a result, I hardly used them.

There was one time when I was in a paper shop and my money was in my back pocket. I reached back and opened my coat, completely revealing my gun and holster. The shopkeeper looked at the gun, then at me, then back at the gun. He just shook his head. I strolled out of the shop, saying to myself, 'You stupid bastard, Harry.'

Back in the woods, the weather was getting colder. It was October now and there was one day in particular when I nearly gave it all up. I was lying under my plastic sheet and it was pissing down and had been for hours. I was soaked right through to the skin and freezing cold. Every single bit of my gear was saturated. I thought, 'Bollocks to this. I'm going to give myself up.' I packed up all my stuff and made my way to the edge of the woods.

As I reached the clearing I looked up at the sky and, all of a sudden, the sun broke through the clouds. The whole place brightened up and I thought, 'No, fuck it.' I turned around and went back to my camp. I strung up a line, hung up all my wet gear and sat down with a nice cup of tea.

Thursday 10th November

I'd been on the run for three months and I needed some more money so I decided to rob a factory that I'd had my eye on for a couple of weeks. I waited until dark and made my way round the back of it.

It was easy enough to get into. Once I was inside I found the safe, an old type called a Milner. These safes were known to be easy to get into from the back, as they were only tinplate, but first I had to prize it away from the wall. I found a big crowbar with a spike on the end. The safe was a big heavy bastard and it took me ages just to budge it an inch. I struggled and struggled with it. I was cursing and spitting but eventually I got it on to its side. I rammed the spike into the back of the safe, expecting it to open, but it didn't. Instead it sent a shiver straight up my arm so hard that I nearly fell over. When I finally got the back of the safe open, I saw two large money bags and I was right chuffed until I went to pick them up. Both of them were filled with silver change. All fucking night I had worked on that safe! For two bags of change! By now it was daylight. I picked the bags up. I could hardly lift the bloody things but they'd have to do.

Friday 11th November

I made my way back to the main road, the A11. The cars were whizzing past and I couldn't take the chance of crossing with my big bags of silver in case someone saw me. So I decided to wait for a while and had a little sleep in a ditch. When I woke up I thought, 'Fuck it, I'll have to take the chance.' As I ran across the road and disappeared into the woods, I thought I was safe.

I walked for a while and was just about to start down the track towards my camp when I happened to glance over my shoulder and saw what I thought was a boy walking his dog. I quickened my pace. When I glanced back I could see it wasn't a boy walking his dog at all. It was a policeman with a tracker dog and he had spotted me. I dropped the sacks of money and took off. I looked back.

The copper had unleashed the dog saying, 'Go get him, boy.' I ran through two meadows and into the woods beyond with the dog right behind me. I ran until I could run no more. I leant against a tree and tried to catch my breath. I could hear the dog running around in the bracken.

I stood still, trying not to breathe. I slowly turned and peered from behind the tree. I could see the copper through the bushes only ten feet away. He was calling to his dog, 'Where are you, boy?'

I thought 'This is it,' then suddenly this bloody great Alsatian dog appeared through the bushes about five feet away from me. He snarled when he saw me. I pulled out my gun, turned sideways and held out my left arm. I thought that as the dog grabbed my outstretched arm I would shoot the fucking thing through the head, then I'd have to 'do' the copper.

They say that dogs can sense danger. Well, this dog must have. It looked at my outstretched arm, made a whimpering sound and scampered off with its tail between its legs. I watched him run through a field, taking the copper with him.

Whenever I made a camp I tried to put myself between a town and a gypsy camp, so if the town people saw me they would think I was a gypsy, and if a gypsy saw me he would think I was a townie. It had been a good cover for me until then. Now the policeman who'd been chasing me made his way to the edge of the gypsy camp where his dog had cornered a young gypsy as I watched from a distance. I saw the policeman lead the young man away. I knew the gypsy would protest his innocence and would be sure to mention the geezer living in the woods nearby, meaning me. This was going to be enough to bring half the London police force down on me. I couldn't risk going back to my camp. I wandered around and found a barn about a mile away. It was full of straw and I decided to stay there. It was, I thought, as good a place as any.

Saturday 12th November

Early the next morning, I went back to the woods. I needed some of my stuff from my camp. I crept through the woods and it was eerily quiet. I waded down a small stream so that any police dogs around wouldn't pick up my scent and made my way around the back of my camp, peering gingerly through the bushes. It was deserted. The soft muddy ground had only dog paw prints. I could see no boot prints. But it was too quiet. Something wasn't right. Then I noticed the flap of my tent was open and I was sure I wouldn't have left it like that.

I was just about to stand up and approach my camp when a policeman came out of my tent. He was heavily armed. I stopped dead in my tracks. He hadn't seen me. I tried to turn slowly without making a sound. As I took a step back, crack, I stood on a twig. I didn't hang about to see if the policeman had seen or heard me. I took off and made my way back to the barn.

Sunday 13th November

I was cold and hungry but I was too scared to leave the barn. I had made myself a good hideout among the bales of straw and had completely buried myself in the middle of a giant stack.

At night, the only sound was the rustling and creaking of many animals scurrying about on the cold hard floor of the barn. The bales were infested with rats. I stayed huddled in the barn all that day and night, too scared to move.

Monday 14th November

I woke up early with a start. I tried to move my legs but they were stiff with the cold. I made a little hole in the straw and peered out. There was no one around. I squeezed through the gap and stretched my aching joints. I thought to myself, 'I could murder a cup of tea.' I was starving hungry, cold and thoroughly pissed off and I knew I couldn't carry on much longer. I thought, 'Fuck it, I'm going into town and going to buy myself some fish and chips.' Once I was in the town, I could see the whole area was rotten with police but I didn't care. All I could think of right now was getting something hot inside me. I walked out of the chip shop, leant against a wall and scoffed it down. It was the best fish and chips I've ever eaten. I popped into a shop and bought a few bits and pieces, tobacco and a bit of grub. After eating, getting caught didn't seem such a good idea so I made my way back to the barn as quickly as I could.

Tuesday 15th November

In the morning I woke to the sound of tractors and men shouting. At first I thought it was just farm workers.

I peered through a little hole that I had made in the straw. I could see a tractor pulling a trailer full of men. They weren't farm workers, they were the London Murder Squad. They looked out of place posing as farmers in their country tweed suits and green wellies. I snuggled down in the straw, not moving a muscle. They came into the barn laughing and joking, and started climbing all over the bales, poking and prodding with their sticks. I didn't move. My heart was pounding so loud I thought they would hear it. Then, much to my surprise, they left. I looked through the hole again to see them climbing back on the trailer and starting off down the lane.

Four times they searched the barn and each time they missed me. From where I was I had a clear view over the fields and woods. I could see the police combing the whole area. For most of the morning I watched them. The whole place was cordoned off. Then I saw two officers, apart from the rest, making their way around the edge of the woods. I watched them getting closer and closer. One of them suddenly left the other and started to make his way towards the barn. I covered my face with straw and laid still. He was a uniformed officer and had just slipped away for a fag.

I felt him climb the bales of straw right beside me. Much to my horror, he sat down and lit a cigarette and, as he put his hand down, he put it straight on my face. I sat bolt upright.

'Who are you?' he said.

I knew there was no sense in trying to lie. The whole place was surrounded and if I started fucking with them I would probably end up getting myself shot. So I said, 'I'm the geezer you're looking for. I'm Harry Roberts.'

He looked at me in disbelief and, dragging on his fag, he said, 'Don't fuck me about, give me your real name.'

'It's Harry Roberts,' I said.

All of a sudden his face changed to one of horror. He panicked and fell straight off the bale of straw. He crashed to the ground and was fumbling to get the gun out of his holster. 'Don't move! – Don't move!' He was shaking so much I thought his gun was going to go off.

I told him, 'Take it easy pal, I ain't got a gun on me', and pointed to my Luger in my hideout.

He reached out and got my gun then started shouting to his mate, 'I've got him! I've got him.'

I climbed down from the straw and put my hands in the air.

I could see the other copper running towards the barn. I turned to look at my captor. Still in a panic, he had fallen arse over head backwards and got tangled in some barbed wire. I went to help him up. 'Keep back! Keep back!' he yelled.

As I looked around, the other copper had his rifle aimed at my head. The first copper untangled himself from the barbed wire and was up on his feet now. Waving his gun towards the entrance, he said, 'Come on, out.' Slowly I walked out with him right behind me. When we reached the other officer, he was calling and waving his arms to a Land Rover that was parked just down the lane with two farmers in it.

The Land Rover pulled up and I was bundled in the back with the two officers. We drove to the edge of the woods. In those days the police didn't have radios, so the two officers needed to inform their colleagues personally that they had me. As we got there, the police were just coming out of the trees. I was shocked by how many there were.

In seconds the Land Rover was surrounded by the Old Bill. Hearing I was inside, all hell broke loose and a policewoman started spitting and screaming at me through the open back of the Land Rover. This seemed to whip the rest of the police into a frenzy and they started beating the soft top of the Land Rover with their sticks. They didn't only hit me, they were also hitting the two coppers who had caught me.

At one point I thought they were going to drag me out and lynch me. The two coppers in the Land Rover with me screamed to the farmers to drive on and we screeched off, leaving the mob of mad coppers behind. We drove around the outskirts of the woods to a mobile HQ. The two officers were right chuffed with themselves and were dreaming of their promotion.

When we reached the mobile HQ I jumped down from the Land Rover and a sergeant screamed, 'He ain't handcuffed!' In their excitement, the two officers had forgotten to cuff me. From the mobile unit I was quickly moved to the local nick at Bishop's Stortford.

When we arrived, I stepped out of the van and a blanket was thrown over my head before going into the building. The officers on either side of me were all but running. They were ramming me into doorposts; other coppers were kicking me in the back while going through to the cells. Once in the cell, they stripped me naked and handcuffed me. Two detectives stayed with me in the cell all the time.

Soon Commander Chitty arrived and I was allowed to get dressed. I was to be taken back to Shepherd's Bush police station under heavy guard. I knew that I would have real bother when I reached Shepherd's Bush nick. I would be in for a good beating, maybe more.

When I got inside the nick the bastards were all waiting for me. I was paraded right through the middle of them. They were growling and snarling, pushing and shoving me. I must admit that, at that time, I feared for my life. Then, just at the end of the corridor, I could see my mum. She was waiting there with a doctor. When I reached her she said, 'They ain't hurt ya, boy, have they?'

I replied, 'No, I'm OK.'

It was good to see my mum. I never thought I'd see a friendly face in that place.

Now Slipper of the Yard took over. I was taken into an interview room and shown the statements of Duddy and Whitney. They had indicated that Lilly was involved. I assured him this wasn't true. I made a deal that I would admit everything if they left Lilly out of it. Slipper had the right hump. He kept asking me, 'Why?' I didn't answer. He got up from his chair, swung open the window and said, 'Listen to these bastards. This is all your doing.' Among the TV and newspapers people who crowded the paths outside were groups of young people singing:

Harry Roberts is our friend,
Is our friend, is our friend,
Harry Roberts is our friend,
He kills coppers!

He slammed the window shut and said to the officers who were standing beside me, 'Take him down and charge him.'

I was charged with 'breaking the Queen's peace' by murdering three police officers.

On 5 December 1966, I appeared at the Old Bailey to stand trial with Jack Whitney and John Duddy. Our trial lasted a week and we were all sentenced to three life sentences, with a recommendation that we serve a minimum of 30 years.

John Duddy died in prison in 1981.

Jack Whitney was released in 1991.

I'm still in prison.

Linda
Calvey

Killers

The newspapers nicknamed her the Black Widow, after the female spider of the same name which eats her partner after mating. She was a hard-faced platinum blonde, a typical gangster's moll, with an insatiable appetite for men.

There was **Micky Calvey** – a flashy armed robber from East London whose life was cut short by a policeman's bullet.

Ronnie Cook – tough and violent, jailed for his part in the Brink's Mat bullion robbery. When he came out he wanted his cut.

Brian Thorogood – he was meant to be her minder but he ended up as her lover.

And, finally, **Danny Reece** – the hitman who couldn't

bring himself to kill.

All four fell under the spell of the Black Widow – and it ended in murder.

Linda Calvey's story of crime begins in December 1978, on a busy Saturday afternoon outside a supermarket called Caters in Eltham, South-east London. It was just after closing time, dead on 6 p.m., when an armoured security van pulled up outside to collect the day's takings. It had been a good day for business and the cash bags were full, carrying £10,000. Just as the guards came out of the supermarket, a 3.5 Rover saloon screeched to a halt in front of the security van. Three robbers jumped out of the car, all carrying sawn-off shotguns. One of the robbers coshed the guard and grabbed the bag of money.

However, following a tip-off, the Flying Squad were lying in wait for them. Detective Sergeant Michael Banks pulled out his .38 Smith and Wesson revolver and shouted: 'Stop, we are armed police!'

The three robbers took no notice. Two of them jumped into the front of their car. Detective Sergeant Banks fired two shots at the car, but missed.

The third robber, 36-year-old Micky Calvey, ran to the getaway car and tried to get in the back. With his gun in his hand and his arm outstretched, Banks yelled another warning: 'Stop, or I'll shoot!'

Micky turned to face the policeman, his sawn-off shotgun still in his hand. Banks fired two shots and Micky Calvey slumped to the ground, dead.

His two accomplices sped off leaving his blood-soaked body in the middle of the road.

The shooting of Micky Calvey made the news bulletins that evening on TV but Linda Calvey missed it. She had no idea that her husband was dead until relatives told her early the next morning. She was devastated, especially with Christmas only two weeks away. At the inquest she screamed at Detective Sergeant Banks: 'Murderer! You have left my little children without a father!'

For Micky Calvey that was the end, but not for Linda. She was bitter and insisted Micky had been shot in the back. She would not let the matter drop and kicked up an almighty fuss, getting an independent coroner's report which clashed with the police stories of how Micky was killed. She started a war with the police, insisting there was a cover up.

Shortly after her husband's shooting, Linda became friends with another gangster, a tough, violent man called Ronnie Cook. Later it was alleged that he was one of the other two armed robbers who got away with the £10,000 from the supermarket.

Cook was married with three children, but he helped Linda to get over her loss. He spent lavishly on her and the pair soon became inseparable. However, it wasn't to last. Ronnie Cook was jailed in 1981, sentenced to 16 years for his part in yet another armed robbery.

Cook was besotted with Linda and could not stand the thought of her being alone so he arranged for a friend, Brian Thorogood, to help Calvey financially.

Thorogood, a former Royal Fusilier, was the next to fall

under the spell of the Black Widow. He and Linda were soon involved in a passionate affair and eventually Thorogood left his wife and set up home with her in Crisp Street, Poplar. Thorogood was also a gangster and by the end of 1985 he had carried out a total of 20 robberies, 16 of them using a sawn-off shotgun.

He was eventually jailed in 1985, for 21 years, only this time he took Linda with him. She was found guilty of conspiracy to commit armed robbery and was sentenced to seven years' imprisonment. It was her first taste of life 'inside'.

With Thorogood in prison, Cook soon learned of the affair that had developed between him and Linda. He was furious and vowed to kill Thorogood if he ever met up with him again. With Linda, however, it was different. He loved her and somehow she convinced him that she was faithful, even having a tattoo put on the inside of her thigh, with the words 'True Love, Ronnie Cook'. Ronnie was suitably impressed, but all the time she was still writing to Thorogood.

Linda served four years of her seven stretch and, by 1989, she was out. She continued to visit both men in different prisons and everything was OK until Cook became eligible for home leave from Maidstone jail in November 1990. Linda knew how violent Cook would become when he discovered the extent of her deception. She also knew that the only way to simplify her rather complicated set of circumstances was to get rid of Cook and free herself of him once and for all.

Together, she and Thorogood hatched a plan. He

introduced her to a man still in prison, by the name of Danny Reece. Thirty-five-year-old Reece, from Stratford, East London, was an armed robber serving 13 years at the Verne Prison at Portland, Dorset. He was due for home leave on the same weekend as Cook.

Linda went to meet Reece at the Verne and it was while she was drinking tea with him in the visitors' hall, under the noses of prison guards, that she asked him to shoot Ronnie Cook for £10,000. He agreed to do the job. Linda made all the arrangements. She would get Cook to her house in King George Avenue by late afternoon in November 1990. Reece would be lying in wait.

As the pair entered the house, Reece duly burst in but when he came face to face with Ronnie Cook he couldn't go through with it. He later gave the police a chilling account of what happened.

> *I couldn't do it. I couldn't kill him. I aimed the gun but at the last moment I shot to the side, hitting him in the elbow. He fell backwards into the kitchen. I stepped forward and again aimed my gun but I froze. I had never killed anyone before. Linda grabbed the gun from me.*
>
> *She screamed at Cook: 'Kneel!' She then pointed the gun and shot him in the head. She yelled at me to get out of the house.*

That was the story of the Black Widow that we all heard and are led to believe is true. However, Linda Calvey paints a different picture.

I made the long journey to meet Linda Calvey at Durham Prison. It's a men's prison but holds 35 women inmates in a prison within a prison. When I arrived Linda was waiting for me. The table was set with her best china.

The platinum-blonde hair had gone. It's now a soft shade of chestnut. We sat down and in a softly-spoken voice the pretty 45-year-old started to talk. This is Linda Calvey's own story, not taken from newspapers or police reports or even idle gossip. She gives her own harrowing account of the events which finally ended with her being sentenced to life imprisonment.

★   ★   ★

It's funny how fate plays such a big part in your life, ain't it? But you never realise it until something happens like losing the one you love. Then you look back and it's all as clear as day. I can see now that, in a way, it's through my Micky that I'm where I am today.

I first met Micky in 1969. At the time I was involved with a married man called Terry. I had been seeing him for something like four years. I was only young, sweet 16, when the affair started and, before I knew it, there I was, four years into a relationship that was going nowhere.

By the age of 20, it was starting to get to me. All the things that Mum and Dad had warned me about were coming true. I started to realise that they were right all along and it was no good. In the four years we had been together I had never met any of his family, or anyone he knew come to that. I was just his little secret. It was the same old familiar story: him telling me he loved me and that he would tell his wife but the time wasn't right. 'Just give me time', he used to say. I wonder how many mistresses have heard that before?

But I was young and I was getting pretty fed up with his broken promises. In those days, I was working as a receptionist at Smithson's paint factory in Whitechapel Road opposite the Blind Beggar pub in the East End. It wasn't much of a job but it was handy because I only lived around the corner in Stepney Way.

All I ever seemed to do was quarrel with Terry. Things came to a head one Thursday night and we had one hell of a row. I had the hump. I'd been with him for four years and nothing had changed – I was still in the same position as day one. I screamed at him and told him I didn't want to see him over the weekend. I needed time to think. I was fed up with the whole thing.

I went to work the next morning and walked around all day with a long face. It was Friday and in the late afternoon I got my wages. I decided to cheer myself up with a new dress. I had seen this right nice little number earlier in the week in a market down the road. It was a bright pink mini dress with a big spotted bow in the front. It sounds horrible now but at the time I thought, 'Oh yeah, beautiful!'

I packed up my things early, got my money and set off. I was walking through the market looking at different things when I bumped into my cousin Patsy and her husband George. George looked at me and said, 'What's up with you, babe? You seem right pissed off.'

'Yeah, I am. I've just come down here to buy myself a new dress, to cheer myself up.' I told them all about the row I'd had with Terry, how he hadn't left his wife yet and I wasn't going to see him over the weekend.

They said I must be mad: 'If he ain't left his wife by now, then he ain't never going to leave her.'

I knew they were right but I didn't want to listen. George said, 'Hang on a minute. If you ain't seeing him till Monday, you ain't doing anything this weekend, are ya?'

I said, 'I suppose not.'

'Well, you are now. One of my friends has just come out of prison after doing an eight stretch for robbing a Marks and Spencer's security van – we're having a party for him.'

I said, 'Oh, I don't know. I don't think I'm up for that.'

George explained that the guy was a bit out of touch. He said that everyone going to the party was either with their wife or girlfriend and that I would be doing him a right favour if I went, then the guy wouldn't feel out of place – otherwise he would be the only geezer there without a bird. 'Me and Patsy have been trying to think of someone halfway decent,' he said. 'He's right nice.' Straight away, I thought he was bound to be rough.

I had never met anyone who had been in prison and, like everyone else, I assumed he would have an IQ of about ten, a broken nose and look like a robber's dog. George laughed and assured me he didn't have a broken nose. He said, 'Come on, you're only 20. You don't want to sit in on a Saturday night! Look, you've got your new dress.' So, eventually, I said yes. I wonder how my life would have turned out if I'd said no.

On Saturday I made the effort to get ready. I put my long blonde hair in rollers, put on my false eye lashes and all the make up and laid my new pink mini dress out on the bed. But my heart wasn't in it. I put on my dressing gown and slumped in the armchair in front of the telly with my mum. I told her I couldn't be bothered to go. I was missing Terry and didn't want to go to the party. 'Well don't go then, girl. I'll make us a nice cup of coffee.' Then, at nine-thirty, the phone rang. It was Patsy.

'Lin, are you ready?' she said, 'The bloke's feeling a mug waiting for ya. Every time the door opens he looks up and says, 'Is that her?' She carried on: 'Don't mug us off. Get your dress on and come down. I've phoned a cab. It's on its way.'

She wouldn't take no for an answer. I ummed and ahhed but, in the end, reluctantly I agreed to go. In the pink dress and a pink and green dog-toothed jacket, at least I looked the business.

The cab came and hooted outside. When I arrived at the pub, the Blue Anchor, I still wasn't sure what I was going to find. As I walked in, I saw George standing at the bar with this tasty-looking bloke. I thought, 'Well, obviously that ain't him, he's too nice.'

At that moment Patsy came rushing over. 'Oh, babe, lovely, you're here.' She took my hand and pulled me over to the bar.

George winked at me. 'Linda, this is Micky. Micky, this is Linda.'

We both smiled at each other and George and Patsy disappeared and left us to it. Neither of us knew what to say. We just stood looking at each other. I told him: 'I don't believe this. I nearly didn't come. I didn't know what to expect. I thought you'd be pug-ugly. But on first impressions, you're bloody handsome.'

He roared with laughter and said, 'Well, I've got to tell you, I've been standing here with my fingers crossed hoping you didn't turn up. I've had George saying: "You wait till you see her." I said to George, "If she's so nice, what's she doing staying in on a Saturday night?" I thought to myself, "She must be a right mutt!" But when you walked in the door, I thought, "Cor, what a result!"'

We hit it off straightaway. We went on to the party and had a right good night. At the end of the evening, I invited him back for coffee. As we walked in, there was my old dad, sprawled out on the settee snoring away. We went into the kitchen and I made the coffee. We started to have a little kiss and a cuddle and he tried to go a bit further. I fancied him like mad but I said no. Then Micky asked me if he could take me out for a drink. I said, 'Yes. Yes please!'

At one o'clock the following day, he pulled up in a cab and took me to the Blind Beggar pub. I felt as if I had known him forever, he was so easy to talk to. We spent the whole day together and went straight out in the evening and had another blinding night.

Wherever we went, people were coming up to him and saying they were glad to see him out. It was great. He was the centre of attraction, almost like a film star. He invited me to his house for tea on Tuesday night. I couldn't believe it! I had only been out with him for the weekend and he had already invited me to his mum's for tea! I'd been with Terry for four years and I'd never met any of his family.

When I told my mum she wasn't exactly over the moon about me going out with a crook. Even though I was brought up in the East End and I had three brothers, I wasn't from a crooked family and that made my mum dubious about Micky but, as she said, 'At least he's single.'

So it was all arranged. Micky would pick me up from work on Tuesday. Come Monday morning I went back to work and I was walking on air all day. I had clean forgotten that Terry was picking me up that night. As I walked out of the factory gate, I heard 'bib–bib–bib' and there was Terry hooting his car horn. I walked over to the car and said, 'Yeah?'

Instantly he got the needle, 'What do you mean, "Yeah?" Get in the car.'

'No, I'm not getting in the car. I don't want to go out with you any more. I met someone else on Saturday night.'

He went mad and we had a right old punch-up in the street. I ended up with the biggest black eye you've ever seen in your life. It was massive. I don't think I've ever seen anyone to this day with a bigger or blacker eye than I had.

On Tuesday night the phone rang and it was my Micky. 'You ready? I'm on my way round.'

I had to be honest so I told him about Terry and the black eye. My Micky was livid. He'd deal with it, he said. But did he still want me to go to his mum's? Yes, of course.

When Micky saw my eye he couldn't believe it. 'When

you said you had a black eye I didn't think you meant one like that!'

That upset me and I didn't want to go but he said his mum had the dinner on and I couldn't let her down, so off we went. When we got to his mum's in Whitethorn Street, Bow, there was only his mum at home. She took one look at me and gasped: 'Oh my God in Heaven! You bastard, Micky, what did you do that for?'

He laughed: 'Mum, I didn't do it, would I hit the girl? I only met her Saturday.'

His mum refused to listen. 'Is this what prison taught you?'

'Mum', he said, 'I didn't do it!'

She turned to me, 'Did he do it?'

I laughed and said no.

'I can't believe that,' she mumbled and went back to the dinner. Then his dad came in.

'Dad, this is Linda.'

'You bastard! You've done this to this girl.' He turned to me. 'Don't you stand for it! How long you known him?'

'Saturday, but he didn't do it.'

His dad gave him a right rucking. 'You're knocking the girl about. You can see that's a fresh black eye. She's only been with you since Saturday, it must have been you!'

'No,' I said. 'It wasn't him.'

'You're just defending him. You're a good girl, you are. Don't you stand for it. I wouldn't stand for my girl coming home with a black eye like that!'

Micky started to get annoyed and then his mum came in with the dinner.

No sooner had we started eating when his sister Maureen came in. She screamed, 'Oh Micky what have you done?'

'I ain't fucking done it!' he said.

Even to this day, his family think he gave me that shiner. Micky said, 'I'm not having this. You're my girl. Me and him will have to sort this out.'

From then on I knew the score. After that me and Micky were inseparable. Within a few months we had moved into one room together in a house in Leytonstone. It wasn't really a room, more like a garage extension. It was horrible, it didn't even have a window, just a big mural painted on the wall with curtains either side, like the one in Hilda Ogden's house in Coronation Street. But we were together, starry-eyed and bang in love and that's what mattered.

Then a cousin of mine told me about a flat around the corner above a launderette. The landlord was an Irishman with one arm. I'll never forget him. He was reluctant to let the flat but when I told him about the mural he laughed and agreed to let us have the flat rent-free, as long as I cleaned the launderette and made sure the door was locked at night. We were happy and it wasn't long before I fell pregnant with my first child.

Eventually, we were evicted from the flat after Micky and his mates were larking about one Saturday afternoon. Some workmen had been doing a job in the launderette, stapling floorboards down with a 'Hilti gun'. They had left the 'Hilti gun' behind and Micky and his mates got hold of it and were firing the small nails everywhere – through the windows, through the floor, one even went through the dry cleaning machine and another just missed a lady's head. The landlord went mad when he heard and threw us out.

We didn't have anywhere to live, so I went back to my mum's and Micky went back to his. Not long afterwards Micky was nicked for robbery and was put away for four years. My world had changed but I knew the type of man Micky was when I became involved with him and I accepted him warts and all!

Good old Mum, she sorted me right out. I got a little flat around the corner in Brady Street, Whitechapel. Mum had to pay £60 key money, which was a lot in those days and the flat was right at the top of one of those old tenement blocks.

I settled in quite well there and, not long afterwards, I gave birth to my daughter Melanie. I couldn't wait to take her to show Micky in Wandsworth Prison and, although he never wanted children, he was over the moon with her. It was on that visit that Micky asked me to marry him. I was so happy. We applied to get married straightaway at Wandsworth Register Office.

The day we got married some spiteful person phoned the prison and said that we weren't getting married at all – it was an escape attempt. They couldn't take any chances so the police re-routed all the traffic. They handcuffed Micky and wanted to put a bag over his head but he wouldn't stand for that. As he was driven out of Wandsworth Prison, he had police at the back, police at the front, and he was only doing four years. You would have thought he was doing 44 years. When he arrived at the Register Office, there were armed Old Bill everywhere. It was complete madness. We weren't allowed any guests apart from my mum, dad and, of course, the baby. As we went in they searched Mum, then they searched Dad, and they even searched the baby! We weren't even allowed any photos.

Micky was brought in, still handcuffed, and the police refused to take them off for the ceremony. It was all over in a matter of minutes. The registrar said, 'You may kiss the bride.'

The screw said, 'Oh no he can't' and then they whisked him off back to the prison. They told my dad: 'Keep up with the van and you can have the last half an hour of the visit back in Wandsworth.' As we came out of the Register Office, there were press and TV cameras everywhere. We climbed into my dad's old blue van and a reporter knocked on the window. 'What have you got to say?'

My dad had the right hump, and said, 'Fuck off, that's what I've got to say,' and we chased off behind the van back to the prison for the last half hour's visit. In all the wrong ways, it was a very memorable wedding day.

That evening it was on the telly and the next day it was in all the papers. It must have been an omen: the start of my marriage was on the news and the end of it was too.

Our marriage was full of ups and downs. Micky was always out on some blag or another and I got used to him being put way. He got nicked a couple more times and did short stretches inside. By December 1978 we had been married for ten years and he'd been inside for much of it. Micky never actually told me he was doing a robbery but I knew that when he said he was out 'working' that's what he meant. It was an unspoken rule – he didn't tell me and I didn't ask. However, the job he took on in December 1978 was different . . .

My Micky always went out for a drink on a Friday night, staying out till late. On this particular Friday night, he came home early and told me he was doing a bit of 'work' the next Saturday.

He'd been in prison from the age of 21 to 28, so he had never learned to drive. It didn't bother him as he liked being picked up and driven about and whenever he was on a bit of 'work', he was always picked up.

All the firms liked working with Micky because, as he didn't drive, he used to compensate by being the 'anchor man'. That meant he would go in and hold the fort while everyone else did the job, got clear and came out. A lot of faces had a lot to say for my Micky. He was really staunch because anchor man was the position nobody wanted, being the last one out!

On the Saturday morning he was getting ready to go on the job. He came downstairs and said he was off. 'I'll be home about six,' he said. I thought it was a bit strange that nobody was coming to pick him up but he just brushed it off by saying he was working with different people. I carried on with my normal day, getting the kids ready and doing a bit of shopping, nothing very exciting, and then I got dinner ready. When he came in, he had a long face. 'No need to ask', I said.

'No', he said, 'We missed it. We're gutted.'

He said that they only missed it by a couple of minutes

and he was furious. 'It's nearly Christmas. I've got to have it. I'm going again next week.'

Now, I knew he didn't like going back on something but he said he was relying on the money for Christmas and he didn't have anything else in the pipeline.

All week, he moped around the house. Come Saturday the same thing happened: he got all ready and off he went. I thought to myself, 'I hope he gets it today, the miserable sod.' I pottered about all day, got the dinner ready as usual. By 6.30 p.m. I heard the door slam. He didn't even speak. He went straight upstairs and when I heard him running a bath, I thought I'd better leave him alone.

Eventually he came down with a face so long he could have tucked it into his underpants. I asked him what the matter was and he just snapped, 'We missed it again.'

I said, 'Perhaps you ain't meant to have it then.'

He got really annoyed at that. 'Never mind I ain't meant to have it. I've got to have it.'

He was going on about how he'd got to get the kids presents for Christmas and how he wasn't going to let it go. He was going again next week. I looked him straight in the eye and said, 'You don't want to go, do you?'

I knew the answer, and he said, 'No, I truly, truly don't want to go. It's a bad bit of work. I've been on it twice already. It's an omen . . . but I've got nothing else.'

I pleaded with him not to go. I said I would ask my mum and dad. I was sure they would lend us a couple of hundred pounds, just to tide us over Christmas but he wouldn't hear of it. He said he wouldn't ponce off my mum and dad, it wasn't on. But he would ask around in the week. A couple of friends owed him. And he promised that if he got back what was owed to him, then he would give the job a miss.

He asked various people but he had no joy. By mid-week he said he was in a corner but he had no choice. He had to go.

I was a bit upset that he'd got knock-backs from people he shouldn't have. Whenever he was flush, he would always help people out. But it was his business.

By the Thursday he got his Giro and said, 'Come on, I'm going to buy you something for Christmas.' We took the kids around to my mum's and set off for the market. We were having a look around and Micky said he wanted to buy me a dress.

We had this standing joke between us, that his favourite colour was lavender. I used to say to him that he would fancy me in a coal sack as long as it was lavender. As we were walking past this shop window, we saw a plain dress with boot-lace straps and a lavender lace bolero. He loved it and made me go in and try it on. While I was in the changing room the assistant told him that it also came in black. When I came out with the lavender dress on, he said it looked blinding, but he said try it on in the black. I laughed. 'It's a waste of time,' I said. 'You know your favourite colour is lavender.' But, strangely enough, for the first time ever, he chose the black instead of the lavender.

'Looks great, sweetheart. Wear it when we go out on Saturday night.' He laughed. 'If I crack it Saturday, I'll buy you the lavender one as well.' When we came out of the shop he insisted that I go and pick the kids up. He said he wanted to go and buy them a few bits for Christmas.

I didn't think he had any more money but he told me just to go home and he'd be back later. So I collected the kids from my mum. A couple of hours later he came home and I couldn't believe it. He had all the Christmas things. I said, 'Where on earth did you get all that?'

He wasn't going to tell me at first but in the end he said that one of his friends, who ran a scam using stolen cheque books and cards, had given him a cheque book and card. This was known as 'kiting' and Micky had never done kiting before, that wasn't his bag, but at least he said he knew the kids would have a decent Christmas.

He bought Melanie an old-fashioned doll's pram with big iron wheels and a wickerwork body. It was lovely; she still has it. And he bought Neil a desk and chair and also lots of bits and pieces for under the tree and all the decorations.

I had been working down the market a couple of days a week and that Friday I was working on a knitting wool stall down in Maidstone market with my mum. When I got home, Micky and the kids met me at the front door. Micky said to the kids: 'Tell Mummy to close her eyes.'

As I walked in, he said, 'Open them. Me and the kids did this for you.' They had decorated all up my hallway and in the front room. He had got all the decorations from the cheques, so there were bundles of them. There was an artificial tree all decorated with fairy lights. It looked like Santa's grotto. You can imagine my kids! They were over the moon that they'd spent all day doing this with their dad. Melanie was eight at the time and my Neil was only four.

On the sideboard were two piles of cards. Micky told me that he had written them all out. One pile was for the family and the other for all his mates inside. He said that all I had to do was stick on the stamps and post them on Monday.

It was a lovely surprise. Everything looked so pretty. We had our dinner and put the kids to bed. When we sat down together later in the evening, things seemed so peaceful. We had all the kids' toys and all the decorations for Christmas. I said to Micky: 'Leave it now, don't go back on that job tomorrow.'

He just looked at me and said, 'No, darling, I can't. I have to go.'

On the Saturday, he came running downstairs all ready to go. He called out: 'I'm off.' A couple of minutes later he was back. He'd forgotten his gloves. He banged on the front door and said, 'Look I ain't coming in. It's pissing hard. I don't want to take my boots off. Just nip up to the bathroom for me. I forgot my gloves.'

As I ran upstairs to get them, my Melanie looked out of the door and saw her dad standing in the doorway. 'Daddy, come in, you're getting all wet.'

I ran back down the stairs, handed Micky the gloves and said, 'Go on then, you don't want to be late.' I gave him a quick peck on the cheek and shut the front door.

All my Melanie had seen was her dad standing in the doorway and later, for weeks afterwards, every time she saw me she shouted, 'You killed my dad! You did! You wouldn't let him in!'

As you can imagine, this slaughtered me. On top of

everything else, my little eight-year-old daughter hated me.

That day, I just went on with things as usual. I dropped the kids off at my mum's as we were going out that night. I got a little bit of shopping in, went home and cooked a lovely roast chicken dinner. By 5.30 I was thinking to myself: 'He'll be home in a minute.' Six o'clock came and went. I thought: 'Sod him, I'll eat my dinner.' I turned the oven right down low and put a plate over his dinner so it wouldn't dry up. I decided to get ready, thinking that by the time I was ready he would be home. I ran a bath, put my heated rollers in my hair and laid my new black dress out on the bed.

I laid back in the bath and smiled to myself. I thought, 'I know what's happened. He's cracked it. He's got the money and he's so relieved he's gone for a drink and got a little bit involved.' I put on my dressing gown and made myself a cup of coffee. By this time it was getting on for 7.30 p.m. and I was just about to switch the telly on when there was a knock at the door. It was Jerry and his girlfriend, the friends we were going out with. They were early.

I opened the door. Jerry must have seen the worried look on my face. Straight away he said, 'Where is he? Is he all right?'

I told him that Micky wasn't home yet. He looked puzzled. 'What do you mean, he ain't home yet?' Jerry knew that my Micky had gone on a job but, like me, he never knew who he went with. Jerry said, 'I don't like the sound of this.'

I was starting to get worried. I explained to Jerry that

maybe he'd cracked it and gone for a drink. 'Yeah, yeah, that's it, babe.' But I knew that he was only humouring me. We decided to go and look for him. There were only four pubs he'd go to. I ran upstairs and put on my new dress. It's ironic that the night Micky died I wore black, because I hardly ever wore black.

We left my house just before the eight o'clock news. If we'd stayed at home we would have seen that there had been an armed robbery in Eltham and one of the robbers had been shot dead. Not that I knew where the robbery was, but I think I would have put two and two together. But I missed it and, apparently, 20 minutes after I went out, the police went to our house to inform me. I missed them too. I bet they were relieved when I wasn't home. Then, I was told later, they went to his mum's, but she's deaf and didn't hear them, so they went on to his brother's. He said he would let me know.

Jerry, me and his girlfriend went off to Micky's favourite pub, the Needlegun, down the Roman Road, which some friends of ours were running at the time. I went straight up to the bar and asked, 'Has my Micky been in?'

The landlady replied, 'No darling, I ain't seen him.'

I told her that if he came in later could she tell him I was looking for him and that I was now going to the Carpenters, another of his haunts. We went to the Carpenters. He wasn't there.

In the end, we did the rounds, but Micky was nowhere to be found. We ended up in a pub in Hackney owned by some friends of ours called Ron and Sylvie. I asked Sylvie if

Micky had been in and she said no but he'd phoned. I was to stay there as he would be back later. In fact, Sylvie had seen the news, and Micky had told her the night before that he was doing a job. She just guessed that it was Micky who had been shot but she wasn't sure. Later she told me that all she could think of saying when I came in the pub looking for Micky was that he'd phoned, just to keep me in the pub with friends. I didn't know any of this at the time. By about 2 a.m. I had the right hump. Micky still hadn't turned up so I decided to go home.

I thought it was a bit strange when I saw Sylvie take Jerry to one side and whisper something to him. Next minute they were all insisting that they come home with me. I said: 'No, Micky will probably be home when I get there.' But they were having none of it and Sylvie insisted on coming with me. When we pulled up in a cab, the house was still in darkness. I couldn't understand it.

We had a cup of coffee and I was moaning away to Sylvie: 'You wait till he gets home.' By this time, it had turned 3 a.m.

Sylvie said: 'Come on, darling, go to bed, get some sleep.'

I got into bed. I wasn't worried any more because Sylvie had said he phoned. I was just angry that he still hadn't come home. I was woken suddenly by the phone ringing. It was Micky's brother, Terry. I said, 'Hello, Terry, bit early for you to ring ain't it? What's up?'

He stuttered a bit, then said, 'Look, I've had the Old Bill on. Micky's been nicked. You'd better come over here now.' He asked who I was with. I told him Sylvie. 'Good,' he said. 'Get a cab.'

I called out to Sylvie: 'Sylv, he's been nicked. We've got to go to his brother's.'

I ran around frantically getting ready. I picked up a few things that I thought my Micky would need. Sylvie took the bag out of my hand and reassuringly said: 'He won't need anything darling, Terry would have sorted that.'

'Yeah, you're right,' I said.

We got the cab to Brabazon Street, Poplar. Terry lived in a tall block of flats and while we took the lift I was chatting away to Sylv. She wasn't saying much. Like a lot of tall blocks of flats built in the sixties, as you open the street door there's a weenie passage, then it turns into a long passage with all the doors off into the bedrooms and lounge.

I reached the front door. Terry was waiting for me. It must have been hard for him. First to phone me with some cock and bull story to get me there and, now he'd got me there, he'd got to tell me.

I walked in and said, 'Well, where is he Tel? What's happened?'

I turned and suddenly thought, 'What are all these people doing in Terry's flat at this time in the morning?' Then I saw my mum and said, 'Hello, Mum, what you doing here?' What was she doing here? It was weird. They were all looking at me. I said, 'What's going on?'

Terry put his arm around me and said, 'Micky's dead, Lin.'

All I can remember is hearing someone screaming and screaming. I was thinking, 'Who's that screaming. Make them shut up.' But it was me screaming.

Someone shouted, 'Slap her round the face. She's hysterical.'

I don't know if anyone did hit me or not. All I can remember is Terry's wife giving me a brandy saying, 'Drink this, darling.'

Slowly, Terry told me what had happened. He said that the police said that Micky had been on an armed robbery and had come face to face with a copper. Micky is supposed to have said, 'It's me or you, copper,' and there had been a shoot-out. The police said they had no choice but to shoot Micky through the stomach and he died.

I screamed at Terry, 'No, Micky wouldn't do that!'

Terry tried to comfort me. He said, 'It's got to be right, Lin. The Old Bill have told me.'

I didn't know what to do. I asked Terry what happened next. He said as I was Micky's wife I had to go and identify his body. We drove over to South London to the morgue. There was a heavy frost that morning and I was freezing cold, but nothing was as cold as the chill I felt as I walked into that morgue. I felt like I was watching someone else do all these things. I was totally numb. As I walked in, I was met by a man holding a piece of paper for me to sign. It was odd, he hardly gave me time to get in the door before he thrust the paper in my hand and snapped, 'Sign here.'

I just looked at him and said, 'Where's my Micky?'

I wasn't going to sign any bits of paper until I knew exactly what had happened. The man took me towards a small window and told me to look through it. A big fat man in a white coat wheeled out a trolley with a white sheet over it. As he approached the window, he pulled back the cover. It was my Micky. Me and Terry started to cry. The man said:

'Is this your husband?'

Quietly I answered: 'Yes.'

'Sign here,' the man snapped again and tapped the pen on his clipboard. I snatched the board out of his hand and threw it on the floor.

How could he be so callous? There was my Micky lying dead on that trolley and all he was interested in was a stupid bit of paper. I knew there was something funny about the whole thing by the way the man was acting.

At the time I was too distressed to be able to put my finger on it, but I was determined to get to the bottom of my Micky's death. As soon as I got home I phoned my solicitor and, with his help, we put up a big fight with the police. They said my Micky was shot in the stomach but I didn't believe them. I told them I wanted an independent post mortem – and suddenly they said the body had been accidentally 'lost'. A few days later, when they knew I wasn't going to give up, they 'found' it again and my post mortem clearly stated that Micky was shot in the back. What was going on? Is that what they were covering up? Afterwards we took Micky home. We wanted him home for the last time so we could say goodbye to him properly. The funeral directors came and laid my Micky out in his coffin in the front room. They told us to turn off all the heating and, during the day, to open the windows. It was very noisy because the council were digging up the road outside and the constant drilling and banging were driving us mad.

Throughout the next couple of days the house seemed full of people, all sorts and some I'd never even met before. They all wanted to pay their respects. All the family was there too, and Maureen, Micky's sister, decided to stay overnight with me. With all the windows open, the house was freezing cold, but Micky's mum came to the rescue and brought us a couple of her nightdresses, the old-fashioned ones made out of white winceyette which came right down to the ground. That night, me and Maureen huddled together to keep warm. I closed my eyes and started to drift off when, all of a sudden, I heard a voice call out: 'Help!'

I sat up and listened. I thought I was dreaming. Then I heard it again: 'Help!'

I shook Maureen. 'Wake up, wake up. Micky's not dead, he's calling me.'

All bleary-eyed, she kissed me on the forehead and said, 'Bless your heart, darling, you're dreaming, go back to sleep.'

'Yeah, you're right, I must have been dreaming.' But as soon as I put my head on the pillow I heard it again: 'Help!'

This time, Maureen heard it too. She sat bolt upright and said, 'Fuck me, you're right.' We grabbed each other's hand and started to make our way downstairs. We were scared stiff and when we got outside the front room door, we started to argue about who was going to go in first. 'He's your brother,' I said.

'Yeah, and he's your husband,' she replied.

We crept in quietly and peered into the coffin. Micky was still in there and he was dead all right. Then, again, we heard: 'Help!'

'Someone's having a fucking game with us,' Maureen said and she ran outside but she couldn't see anyone.

'Help!'

She went outside the front gate and looked down into a big hole that the workmen had been digging. She peered over the top of it and a drunken man was lying there shouting, 'Help!' When he saw her, he screamed his head off and scampered out of the hole.

The next day, the man's wife came over and apologised. She said, 'I'm sorry – all he saw was this figure above him, peering at him, dressed in a long white robe. He thought you was a ghost!'

My Micky was shot on 9 December 1978 but I wasn't allowed to bury him until 8 January 1979. His funeral made the front page of all the newspapers and over 200 people came to show their respects. Everyone liked my Micky. In February I went to the coroner's and heard the jury's verdict: 'justified homicide'.

All the police who'd been involved in the shooting of my Micky were congratulating each other in court as if they had won a prize in a raffle. Detective Sergeant Banks, the officer who had shot him, even received a commendation. I couldn't believe it, what a liberty! I couldn't hold back my anger any longer. I walked up to Detective Sergeant Banks, slapped him hard around the face and shouted at him: 'Show my kids the commendation you got for killing their father.'

It wasn't right that he should be allowed to get away with killing my Micky then say all those things. By this time I was exhausted. All that had happened affected me badly. I became bitter and nothing seemed to matter anymore. Part of me died when I buried my Micky and so did my respect for the police and the authorities.

When a villain is put in prison or, as in Micky's case, dies, the first thing that happens is that the 'firm' put on a benefit night. They raise a bit of money to help out the family and it was at Micky's benefit night in the East End that I met Ronnie Cook again. We already knew each other. Once he'd come around to pick my Micky up early one morning while I was cooking breakfast. I opened the door and there stood this tough, athletic-looking man dressed in a track suit. He came in and I cooked him egg on toast.

On the benefit night, he came up to me and gave his condolences and asked if it would be OK if he came around to see me the next morning. I said yes; I didn't think anything of it. The next morning he came to the house and gave me some money and said that if I needed anything, anything at all, I just had to ask.

Over the next couple of months I went a bit wild. Every night I went out drinking and everywhere I went I kept bumping into Ronnie Cook. We hit it off right from the start and it was strange really, because he was the exact opposite of my Micky. They were like chalk and cheese.

Micky was always flamboyant, extrovert, smart, the man about town. Ronnie was very quiet and soberly dressed. People were wary of him. He had a reputation for being a hard man and nobody messed with him. I liked that but with me he was always kind and gentle. He always seemed to have money and he started bringing me lots of presents. My Micky was a robber but he wasn't in Ronnie's league. Ronnie was a top-of-the-tree robber, into heavy blags.

Over the next two years my life changed. I wanted for nothing, Ronnie made sure of that. He never gave me large lumps of money but he took care of all my bills. He bought me the best clothes money could buy and my kids never went without.

Ron left his wife and moved in with a friend of his but I saw him every day and we went out most nights. Slowly, almost inevitably, I fell in love with him.

At my trial the police said that the motive I had for killing Ron was that I wanted his money. That was a joke. With Ron alive I never wanted for anything, but Ron was shrewd. He used to spread his money about and invested the bulk of it in legit businesses. On the day that Ron was arrested for the Brink's Mat bullion raid, he had given me £20 to get his suede cardigan out of the cleaners. That was the only money I had of Ron's.

While Ron was away on remand, my life changed again drastically. No Ron, no money and I had to sign on. My standard of living dropped and I found myself not being able to pay my bills. Ron was worried about me and when I went to see him in prison, he gave me the phone number of a friend of his called Brian Thorogood. 'Phone him,' Ron said. 'Tell him I want to see him.'

I phoned the number and spoke to Brian. I told him Ron wanted to see him on a visit with me. He didn't want to go with me but I told him Ron insisted. Instinctively, he didn't like me and I didn't like him, but he came with me to see Ron who said, 'I want her looked after. I want my shares of the company put in her name.' Brian wasn't happy. He tried to reason with Ron but Ron wasn't having any of it. 'Just do it,' he said.

He also told him to give me £100 straightaway, and then to bring me money every week out of the firm. He was to drop it off every Friday. I was a bit embarrassed by all of it but I knew not to say anything and mug Ron off, so I just sat back and said nothing.

Brian handed me £100 and, after that, every Friday, regular as clockwork, he arrived at my house and paid me. He had been asked to look after me and that's exactly what he did.

Soon after that Ron got me up on a visit. He arranged for me to go to work at Brian and Jimmy Western's firm, J.T.Ws in Grays, Essex. It was all legit, he said. Brian was going straight now and I wouldn't have any more worries. Brian would take care of me. Ron said it wouldn't be for long and as soon as he was out he would take care of me himself. Poor Ron, he was so sure he would get a not-guilty verdict for his part in the Brink's Mat raid. He even said he had paid off some of the jury. He said it was a sure thing so when he got a guilty verdict and was sentenced to 16 years, neither of us was prepared. We were both stunned.

On the first visit I had with him he was understandably depressed. 'Listen, darling, I'm not going to be getting a day off sixteen years. I know I've got to do at least ten and I'll understand if you say no to what I'm going to ask you.'

I couldn't think what he was going to say. I was still reeling with the shock of him getting 16 years. Then he asked me to wait for him. He didn't mind if I had affairs. 'Just don't flaunt it,' he said. 'Be there for me every visiting day. Look pretty for me, that's all I ask.' He told me to think about it. 'I know I've got no right to ask it of you . . .'

Well, he had every right, I didn't hesitate. I told him I would wait for him. I didn't lie to him. I couldn't promise him I wouldn't have a boyfriend while he was away but I wouldn't mug him off.

Later I found out that it was the norm for gangsters' wives to have boyfriends while their old man was away but as soon as the husband came out of prison the boyfriend had to go. It was the unspoken rule. As long as you didn't mug them off, it was OK.

I went to work at Brian's firm. I even got my Micky's sister Maureen a job there too and the more time I spent with Brian, the more I liked him. We started to grow very close. He eventually left his wife and moved in with some friends in Hornchurch, Essex. I went straight to the prison and told Ron. He was OK about it. As far as he was concerned we had a deal and so long as I stuck to my side of the bargain and didn't mug him off, things were all right.

Things were fine for a while – until Brian's business went into liquidation. Ron stepped in to help again and I went to work for another company called Colports – he had a share in that company too. However, the money wasn't so good and Brian started to go back out on armed robberies. I knew what he was doing and sometimes I would go with him. My job was to 'case' the post offices and to time the security vans making their deliveries.

In 1985, I was eventually arrested and charged with conspiring to rob two post offices, along with Brian, two other friends of ours, my brother Tony and his wife Sandra. I was given bail but Brian was sent to Brixton Prison as a Category A prisoner. I used to go and visit him most days and, because he was on remand, I was allowed to take him a home-cooked dinner. It was while I was visiting Brian that he told me about this young bloke he had met in there. His name was Danny Reece.

Brian told me that he was young and hot-headed but he was a real nice bloke and would I do him a dinner sometimes as well! I didn't mind, it wasn't any hardship for me, so that's what I did. After a while, Danny would occasionally come out and sit with us on a visit . He was really nice, a big strong man and very good looking. All this carried on for 15 months until my trial.

On the day of my trial, I was nervous. I had never been on trial myself before. I had been lots of times with my Micky but it's a different kettle of fish when you're in the dock yourself. I appeared at Southwark Crown Court and pleaded not guilty.

Our trial lasted three weeks. They found Brian guilty of 21 armed robberies and sentenced him to 21 years of imprisonment. Carl, our friend, was found guilty of nine armed robberies and given 14 years. My brother got nine years. Then it was my turn. I was found guilty and given a seven-year prison term. I couldn't believe it. Me! Seven years! I was taken to Holloway Prison and it was a complete culture shock. I had never been in prison before and I didn't know what to expect. It came as a big blow, like someone had smacked me in the face.

The first letter I got in Holloway was from Danny, saying how sorry he was that I had been put away. The second letter I got was from Ron, saying how upset he was. He told me to tell the governor that I was his common-law wife and apply for internal visits, which I did but it was seven months before I was taken to Gartree top security prison to see my Ron. I was as nervous as hell going to see him. As far as Ron was concerned, he'd trusted Brian to look after me. He was even OK about us being together, but Brian wasn't flavour of the month. I knew from Ron's letters that he blamed Brian for getting me involved.

It wasn't like the papers and the police tried to make out. They said that Ron had the needle about me seeing Brian. That wasn't the case at all. For a start, I could never have had the affair with Brian if Ron didn't say it was OK. What Ron had the hump about was that Brian got me nicked.

I was driven to Gartree Prison in Market Harborough, Leicestershire. I knew Ron was annoyed. I didn't know how he was going to react to me. When I got there I was taken into the men's reception room. The visits at Gartree are held in the main hall, with all the other visitors. However, as I was a prisoner too, I had to go into the male prisoners' waiting room. I was really embarrassed sitting with them, waiting to go in. All the prisoners were kind to me though, saying, 'Come on girl, you'll be all right.'

As I walked into the visiting hall, all the other visitors were looking up, waiting anxiously for their husband or boyfriend to come out. When I came out of the prisoners' door wearing my blue towelling track suit, they all seemed to be looking at me and the thought went through my mind, 'I bet they think I'm a transvestite.' Ron was waiting for me with newspaper clippings under one arm and a box of chocolates under the other. He never was a kiss and cuddly person but when I walked over to him he gave me a kiss on the cheek. Then he growled a bit and said, 'How do you think I felt? Men do bird for armed robbery, not women.'

I told him I was sorry, I didn't mean to mug him off but he wasn't angry with me, he had the raving hump with Brian for involving me. He sat all the way through the visit with the box of chocolates under his arm. Just as I was leaving he said, 'By the way, these are for you. Do you still love me?'

I laughed and said, 'I never stopped loving you, you silly bastard!'

I continued to visit Ron every three months and eventually he was moved to Maidstone Prison in Kent. Soon after, I was moved too, to Cookham Wood, also in Kent. All the time I was writing to both Ron and Brian. I was mixed up. I didn't want to let Ron down – or Brian. And then there was Danny . . .

Through letters we'd become very close. I told him that I felt he'd become another brother to me. There was a special bond between us. I'd ask his advice and he'd ask mine. He told me how he and his wife had split up and all about his three sons. While he was in prison his eldest son had been run over and killed and Danny was distraught. I felt sad for him and I started writing to him even more. By a strange coincidence, his son was buried in the same cemetery as my Micky, just 200 yards away. I promised Danny that, when I was released, I would put some flowers on the boy's grave for him. I tried to comfort him. I told him, 'he'll know they're from you.'

When I was released I continued to visit Ron in Maidstone Prison. I never went to visit Brian, but visited Danny instead. I did as I promised and put some flowers on his son's grave and that made him happy. I told Ron all about visiting Danny. He didn't mind at all as he had much more important things on his mind. By now Ron was on his way out from Maidstone. He'd got the job of cleaning the hostel attached to the nick. That meant that, once he had cleaned the place, he had the rest of the day to himself and didn't have to return to the nick until eight o'clock at night. He would often ring me and we would go for a drink or a meal or, as increasingly happened, I would bring him home.

Ron didn't have much longer to serve. He was due out on 19 December 1990. He'd left his money with 'friends' to look after but now he was coming home he wanted it back. That wasn't so easy. The 'friends' he'd left it with wouldn't, or couldn't, give it back to him.

Ron was furious and said that he would take care of them if he didn't get his dough back. Everybody knew that Ron meant what he said and that he was more than capable of doing it. His 'friends' had no choice: they either had to give Ronnie back his money or they had to kill him.

Danny had moved to the Verne Prison at Portland, Dorset and I went to visit him. He was so happy. He'd just heard that he had got home leave and the first thing he was going to do was catch a train and go and see his son's grave. I knew how upset he was over the boy. I couldn't let him catch a train and go on his own so I insisted that I pick him up and take him. I also knew that he didn't have any up-to-date clothes to wear when he came out and he was really embarrassed about it. I understood what that was like because I'd felt the same when I came out of prison. So, when I got back, I bought him a black suede jacket from a hoyster and a smashing silk shirt. When I gave them to him he was choked up. Danny is a proud man and it was hard for him to accept them from me. I told him to think of them as a gift but he insisted that when he got himself straight he would pay me back.

On the Friday morning that Danny was coming home, I got up early for my long drive down to Dorset. I was excited about Danny coming out. My friend Ashley had agreed to come with me for the ride, so I picked her up on the way.

We pulled up in the car outside the prison and waited for Danny. It was a freezing cold November day, the car heater was full on and I wiped the mist from the windscreen with my woolly glove. When we saw Danny come out of the big gate, we both jumped out of the car and gave him a big kiss and a cuddle. It was good to see him free for the first time since I had met him.

We stopped on the way for breakfast and again to pick up a wreath and when we got to the cemetery Danny was beside himself with grief. He threw himself on top of the grave and sobbed.

I was choked. I didn't know what to say. I didn't have any words to comfort him. Ash and I turned and walked away and waited for him in the car. He seemed to stay at the grave forever. When he got back in the car, none of us said a word. I just drove him home. We went to his mum's house and I asked him if he fancied going out for a meal that night. He said yes but, more than anything, he would like a home-cooked roast dinner.

That was even better, I thought. Later that day Ash and I bought a chicken and Ash put it in the oven while I went to collect Danny at eight. We all had a drink and a lovely meal and that's how Danny's fingerprints were in my house – just three people enjoying each other's company, nothing more sinister as the police later tried to make out.

On the Sunday morning me and Ash had just come back from buying the shellfish for Sunday's tea from Chapel Market when the phone went. It was Ron. 'Fancy a drink darling?'

Ron was always good company and we arranged to meet at his favourite pub, the Bun House, later that day. When I got there Ron was already in the bar. We had a great afternoon, drinking and laughing. It was fun and the following day Ron was being allowed out again so I said I'd pick him up first thing. I was looking forward to spending more time with him. We came out of the pub at four o'clock. A friend drove Ron back to Maidstone Prison and I drove off back to North London.

The next day Ron was waiting at the door of Maidstone Prison as I drove up. He waved, then ran back inside and brought out a big bag of photos to give to me. He was clearing his cell out, getting ready for going home in a couple of weeks' time. He got in the car, I kissed him and we drove off. Halfway home I stopped for petrol and Ron said he would drive the rest of the way. So I moved to the passenger seat and looked at the photos that I had sent him over the years.

We pulled up at my house which was in a cul-de-sac facing a park. You had to drive to the end of the cul-de-sac to turn around and, as Ron turned the car, I looked around. I noticed a man and two ladies unloading their shopping on to the pavement. I could also see a policeman walking around the edge of the park.

Ron handed me the front door keys and I asked him to bring the milk in from the doorstep. We had just walked into the kitchen when the front door burst open and a man shouted, 'Get down, Police!'

Ron turned and said, 'What's up, mate?'

In an instant, the man, who was dressed all in black, fired, hitting Ron in the elbow and knocking him off balance. Ron staggered back into the kitchen. It was like slow motion. I didn't even see the gun. It was either in a bag or wrapped up in something.

I saw blood seeping through Ron's pale blue bomber jacket and I screamed and put my hands over my face. Then

I cowered in the corner. Within seconds, I heard another deafening bang. I closed my eyes tight and hid my face. I was so scared. The next time I looked up the man had gone. Slowly, I stood up, trying not to make a sound. I looked at Ron. He was covered in blood.

I felt I couldn't breathe and I gasped for air. I didn't know what to do. I rushed to pick up the phone, then remembered the policeman in the park. The front door was wide open and I ran out and started screaming. The man and the ladies I'd seen earlier, unloading their shopping, came running over. I was hysterical and pointed to the house. One of the women was a nurse and she and the man rushed inside. I tried to tell the man what had happened but I wasn't making any sense. I screamed at him to get the policeman in the park and he ran off to get him. The woman came back out of the house and also ran off towards the park, to tell the policeman that Ron was dead.

I went back inside and there was blood everywhere, my Ron's blood. He just lay there still, unrecognisable, with half of his head missing. In blind panic, I screamed at him: 'Get up Ron! Get up!' But he didn't move. He was dead. I was in a state of shock. I tried to answer the police questions as best I could. I told them everything that I could remember but I had a mental block. It had all happened so quickly.

At first, the police were all right with me. Then they found out that I was Linda Calvey, the wife of Micky Calvey, the armed robber who had been shot by one of their own. The Linda Calvey who had kicked up such a stink about Micky's death. After that their attitude changed towards me.

They started looking for a motive for me murdering Ronnie. They wanted it to be me.

Two and a half weeks after Ronnie was shot, the police arrested me and charged me with murder. I couldn't believe it. Then they arrested Danny. They said he'd confessed that, together, we'd hatched the plan to kill Ron and that it was me who fired the fatal shot.

I knew that was crap. Danny did not say that. Why should he? But the police were adamant that I did it. I found out later what had happened. The police had interviewed Danny in prison. He told them he'd never met Ron, that he knew he was my long-time boyfriend and that I was looking forward to having him home after all those years. Nevertheless, they charged him.

They didn't stop there. They accused Ashley's boyfriend Billy Francis of being the getaway driver. If it hadn't been so serious it would have been laughable – he only drove a Y-reg Yugo! They charged another man, Billy Swan. They even charged my daughter Melanie.

All these charges were later dropped but they pressed the ones against me and Danny. A police officer claimed that Danny had confessed but it's simply not true. Danny has never said he did it – or that I did it. Think what you like but I'm telling you – Danny and I are innocent. The police stitched us up. I couldn't believe the way things were twisted in court. All the way through my trial, I never heard one statement in which Danny said that I did it.

The whole police case revolved around the statement of the woman who lived next door to me, Mrs Saville. She said that she had heard a woman's voice shouting, 'Oh no, Neil,' and then the sound of gunfire. She thought the voice belonged to me.

She went on to say that she then looked out of her window and saw me talking to a man before he ran off towards the park. The second time she looked out of her window, she saw a policeman and two women and a man hurrying towards my house. Well, she was right, she did see all those things but they were twisted around to make it look like I was involved in Ron's murder. They said I shouted, 'Kneel, kneel'. But Mrs Saville was right, I was shouting out: 'Oh no, Neil!', which is my son's name.

I was scared that my son might have been upstairs in the bedroom and that the gunman had gone after him. When Mrs Saville saw me talking to the so-called killer, I was talking to the man who had been unloading his shopping, before he ran to get the policeman in the park.

On the second occasion when she looked out of her window and saw the three people heading towards the house that was right because the lady who had attended to Ron had run to the park as well.

At the trial it all sounded different. We had shit publicity in all the papers saying, 'Danny said she did it.' We didn't stand a chance. Our trial was in Court 1 at the Old Bailey. It lasted six and half weeks but the jury couldn't reach a verdict. The judge sent them out again and told them a majority decision would do.

After two days they came back and said they had a majority of 11–1. The foreman of the jury stood up and the judge said, 'How do you find the defendants. Guilty or not guilty?'

He replied, 'Guilty, your honour.'

I was stunned. I felt as if I had been punched in the face by Mike Tyson. I hadn't thought for a minute, not for a single moment, that they would find me guilty. When the judge sentenced me to life imprisonment, I can only describe it as going to the doctor with a cold and him telling you you've only got four weeks to live. The horror and disbelief knocked me for six.

I looked at Danny. He'd got life too and he had tears in his eyes. He said, 'These tears are for you, not me.'

I held Danny's hand tight as they led us down to the cells and at the bottom Danny hugged me and said, 'We will never give up. We will prove your innocence.'

They took Danny one way and me the other. The newspaper headlines the next day read, 'The Black Widow showed no emotion when she was given life.' No emotion? What did they know? Inside I was dying.

Colin
Richards

Killers

The skies blackened as a severe thunderstorm started. Six stone-faced pallbearers, officers from the Essex police force, carried the coffin through a 200-strong guard of honour into Chelmsford Cathedral. The coffin was draped with the Union Jack and, on top, were laid wreaths of red and white carnations and the officer's blue uniform cap. His widow Susan, 37, herself a former police officer, walked solemnly behind wearing a black velvet suit. Pale but dignified, she was clutching the hand of her ten-year-old son David.

Loudspeakers relayed the service to the scores of people who were outside, lining the pavement in the pouring rain, and standing in the arched doorway of the Cathedral was Sergeant Mervyn Fairweather, 39, who had been shot in the same incident. A large shotgun pellet had lodged in his groin and would stay there for the rest of his life. He closed his eyes and bowed his head as the coffin of his friend and colleague, PC Brian Bishop, was slowly carried past.

PC Bishop, 37, was six feet six inches tall and dubbed 'Captain Courage' by his colleagues because of his outstanding bravery. He had taken five days to die of appalling head wounds. There had never been any hope of his recovery from the first time he was seen by doctors.

Six hundred people were in the congregation at his funeral and all heard the Chief Constable of Essex, Mr Robert Bunyard, say, 'PC Bishop epitomised all that was best in the British bobby. He continued: 'The rules are dangerous; we are obliged to give a gunman the first shot.'

The man accused of murdering PC Bishop was 35-year-old Colin Richards. The boss of an all-purpose discount store, he had turned to a life of crime to save his ailing business.

Richards, a well-respected member of clay pigeon and shooting clubs, also collected guns. He had about 200 of them, all legally held, but neither his well-to-do shooting friends nor even his elegant wife Patricia dreamed that he was also the motor-cycle bandit who had been terrorising the county for months.

The gun-crazy businessman had swapped his pin-striped suit and briefcase for a stocking mask and a sawn-off shotgun to attack banks, building societies and post offices. In his two-year reign of robbery, he netted £30,000 until it all came to a terrifying end on 22 August 1982.

On that day, at 4.20 p.m. Richards pulled the stocking mask down over his face and walked into the post office at Walton on the Naze in Essex, brandishing a sawn-off shotgun, and demanded money. After the raid, he jumped on to a motor-cycle and escaped with £8,705.

Twenty minutes later the Jekyll and Hyde robber went into another post office, this time in Frinton on Sea, and again demanded cash but the cashier pressed the alarm and Richards fled empty-handed.

The police gave chase and he had no choice but to hide the proceeds in bushes at Frinton on Sea. Later that day, at about 7.45 p.m., Richards returned to the lonely seaside road to collect his haul. However, eight armed officers lay in wait and they saw Colin return from the bushes carrying a black plastic bag.

PC Bishop, armed with a revolver, approached Richards and warned him to give himself up. But Richards ignored the warning. Instead, he turned, lifted the black plastic bag containing a sawn-off shotgun and opened fire. PC Bishop took the full force of the blast in the head. Bishop's colleague, Sergeant Fairweather, was hit in the groin. This time, Fairweather managed to fire back with his revolver. After another warning, the other officers opened fire, hitting Richards in the arm, side and back.

The barrage of bullets spun him around and he dropped to the ground. He would never walk again. The bullets paralysed him for life. Later, in the local hospital, a small private ward was turned into a courtroom. Richards, from Brentwood, Essex, lay in bed as ten people crowded into the

15 by 12 foot room. A hospital sister stood beside him as the clerk read the charges. He was accused of:

1. Murdering PC Brian Bishop on 22 August 1983 and attempting to murder Sergeant Mervyn Fairweather.

2. Robbing Walton Post Office.

3. Assaulting Eric Jonathan Cobden with intent to rob at Frinton 22 August.

4. On 27 August 1982, at the Woolwich Building Society, Chelmsford, stealing £6,551.

5. On 1 March 1983, in Romford, stealing £3,877 in cash, the property of Lloyds Bank.

6. Lastly, on the same day in Romford, possessing a sawn-off shotgun with intent to endanger life.

For Colin Richards it was the end not only of his reign of terror but also of life as he had known it. This is Colin's story.

★　★　★

I've always been a bit of an entrepreneur. I've always been willing to try any kind of business and I've always been ambitious. I have qualifications – five O Levels – and in many ways, I suppose I take after my father. He was an intelligent man and he always ran his own business. He had a factory making concrete carriages in Essex, and ever since I can remember it was expected that I would follow in his footsteps and eventually take over the running of the factory. I was never very keen – maybe simply because it was expected of me. I wanted to make my own way, to be a success in my own right. But I did try. I worked for two years in the engineering department of the factory but soon knew it wasn't for me. When my father decided to close down the Essex factory and move lock, stock and barrel to Norfolk, I grabbed my chance to tell him I wasn't going with them.

I was only 19 years old, shy and withdrawn and, anyway, I could never have taken over a factory at that time, I didn't have the confidence or the experience. It didn't go down too well with my father.

My father and I didn't see eye to eye at the best of times. I was young and had other ideas. I had this fancy notion of owning my own garage, God knows why, maybe I just wanted to prove something to him. Eventually, I got my own way and went to Chelsea College and studied for a degree in auto-engineering.

I loved it. I was there for two years and I passed my City and Guilds and all the degrees with flying colours.

I went straight from college into a garage, where a friend of my father's gave me a job. I learned the basic ground rules of running a garage but it didn't take me long to discover that the garage game wasn't for me. There are too many sharks and crooks in that business.

So, after two years, I left and, over the next couple of years, I had various jobs. I renovated an old cottage, exposing all the wooden beams and restoring it to its former glory. I did a bit of this and that, the same as everybody else really. I got married to a smashing girl called Patricia and had a couple of kids, two boys. By the late 1970s, I was working in a wine bar. It wasn't bad money but only just enough to survive and that wasn't enough for me. I wanted to own my own business. I didn't want to work for someone else. I didn't want to do all the work and for someone else to reap all the benefit. That wasn't how I was brought up. Then one day I was walking to the wine bar to start my shift and I noticed a shop for sale. It was an all-purpose discount store, selling everything from hair spray to garden furniture. I didn't know the first thing about the retail trade but it was being sold as a going concern and it took my fancy. I had managed to put a little bit of savings aside for a rainy day and, if I went to my father, I was sure he would help me. I had made up my mind. I was going to buy that shop.

I went to see my father. He wasn't happy about it and it took a huge row before he agreed to help me financially and, even then, he had to add that I wouldn't make anything out of the shop or my life. Bloody cheek. Typical dad. I was determined to prove him wrong. I put all my savings in and bought the shop. I was in business at last!

At first it was OK. But when the manager left after about a year, I hadn't got a clue. I took on a manageress but she didn't have a clue either. Things started to go wrong and the shop started to lose money in a big way. I was working all the hours God sent, but it didn't seem to matter how hard I tried, the shop lost money hand over fist.

I was in a no-win situation. I couldn't sell the shop as I would lose all my investment but I couldn't make any money either. I cut back buying stock and laid off staff. I tried just about everything. I was getting to the end of the road and desperation was setting in when, one evening, I was sitting at home in front of the TV, with a can of beer and a takeaway on my lap. I was staring at the TV but I wasn't watching it. My mind was miles away, thinking about my financial problems. Something dragged my concentration back and I started to watch the programme that was on. It was *Crimewatch*. The presenters were talking about an armed robbery that had taken place. Suddenly it dawned on me. That's it! That's what I could do! Why not? If I could do a robbery, that would be the answer to all my problems. I pushed my cold dinner to one side and stared at the TV, watching the reconstruction of every move the robbers made. I thought to myself, 'I could do better than that'. If only … No, what was I thinking of, of course I couldn't, could I …?

Over the next couple of months, things at the shop got worse. I tried and tried to get the business straight but it was no good. I couldn't ask my father for any more help as he had already given me the money to buy the shop and, anyway, he'd always said I would never amount to anything.

I desperately wanted to prove him wrong, but I knew it was only a matter of time before I went under. Sometimes at night I would just lie in bed staring at the crack in the ceiling, dreaming about doing the perfect robbery.

Every Thursday night, regular as clockwork, I'd watch *Crimewatch*. I'd watch intensely, thinking the robbers always made such stupid mistakes. I convinced myself that I could do better. I was becoming obsessed with doing the perfect robbery. No matter how hard I tried, I couldn't get it out of my mind. I suppose, in desperation, I started to turn my dreams into reality.

I was already a member of several shooting clubs, mainly clay pigeon, so I already had my own guns. One night, I got my double-barrelled shotgun and sawed the barrel down. I scrubbed off all the numbers and identifying marks. I started to watch banks and building societies, trying to get an idea of their routine. I decided that whichever one I robbed would have an alley down the side for an easy getaway. Sometimes I would watch places for hours, occasionally I would actually go into the building society with my gun, then I would just bottle out and go home. This went on for about a year and a half.

On 26 August 1982, I was called up for jury service at Chelmsford Crown Court. I was delighted because the case was an armed robbery. I sat in the corridor in my smart navy suit, waiting to be called in. All the time I was thinking, 'If only I could do it, if only I had the courage …'

When my concentration was broken by the clerk of the court telling me that I wasn't needed after all I was angry but most of all I was disappointed. By now it was two o'clock and I had wasted the whole day. I stepped out of the court house into the bright sunshine and made the decision there and then that was to change my life. I was going to do it! I was going to do an armed robbery!

I walked around Chelmsford town with the sole purpose of finding somewhere to rob. I saw the Woolwich Building Society and it had a small alleyway running down the side. It was perfect. I hurried home. I made up my mind that the very next day I was going to rob that building society. It was 27 August, my birthday. All that night I couldn't sleep, I kept churning my plan over and over in my mind.

I was up early the next morning to prepare everything to perfection. I got some false number plates made up for my own car – what a twit, I didn't even consider stealing a car! I bought a long, brown, greasy-looking wig and stuffed small pieces of rubber up my nose and in my cheeks to make my face look fatter. I wrote a note saying: 'HAND OVER THE MONEY – AND NOBODY WILL GET HURT'.

All day I paced about. This was it. I was going to do it, really going to do it. I felt nervous but also excited. I waited until it was nearly closing time before I walked into the Woolwich Building Society holding my sawn-off shotgun and a carrier bag. As they were just about to close, there weren't many people in there. I walked up to the counter and pushed the carrier bag against the window so the cashier could see my gun. I handed him the note. I didn't say a word. I just stared at him. (Mind you, I couldn't have said a word even if I had wanted to, what with all that bloody rubber in my mouth!) My heart was pounding so hard I could see my chest heaving.

I was in such a state of panic anything could have happened. Maybe the cashier sensed that. He didn't argue. He stuffed the money into the bag that I handed him and I ran out.

In blind panic I forgot to take the note back but I couldn't think straight. I jumped into my car, throwing the money and my gun on to the back seat. I rammed the car into gear and sped off, spitting the rubber out of my mouth as I was going along.

As I drove out of town I could hear alarm bells ringing in the distance. I passed a police car with its flashing lights, driving at top speed, heading towards the town. Adrenalin was rushing around my body – what a high! I couldn't believe I had actually done it! I drove to a quiet spot and my hands were shaking as I counted the money. I had £6,000!! Brilliant!!

The very next day I put the money into the bank, into my business account. I felt a bit guilty, as if people knew. But at least now I could get my business straight. For a while it got me out of trouble but less than six months later I was in trouble again.

I started to think, 'Well that was quite easy. If I did one more, just one more and got a good one then I would pack it in and that would be it.'

I looked around for a suitable building society and got myself ready as before. Only this time things didn't go so good. Oh, I got away all right but when I looked in the bag, I had only got £150. That was no bloody good. I had to put plan B into action. And plan B was to try a bank.

But plan B proved difficult. I tried to rob a couple of banks but they were even harder than building societies. In one bank when I went in waving my gun about, all the cashiers laid face down on the floor behind the counter and refused point blank to give me a penny. I tried about three banks in all but found banks so difficult. Sometimes I would stand outside all day just watching it and plucking up the courage to go in. Then I would bottle out and go home for my tea. Things weren't going to plan. All I needed was one big one, just one, then I could get the business back on its feet and I could stop robbing banks.

My problem was solved by chance one day when I was buying some stamps at the post office and I noticed the cashier's drawer was full of money. With me being in the retail trade, I recognised the five pound notes folded into bundles of £500. My eyes lit up. Yes! I thought, 'I'll try a post office!'

I did, and to my delight I got £9,000 on my very first job. I should have stopped then but I couldn't. I had become addicted to the easy money.

While I was on my way to work one morning, I heard on the car radio that there had been a robbery at the post office in Hornchurch and then the cheeky buggers had robbed another post office about half a mile away. Two in the space of an hour.

'What a bloody good idea,' I thought. ' (A) I could get more money and (B) it would confuse the police.' However, I would have to go out of the Brentwood area; things were getting too hot. I had nearly been caught on a couple of occasions. Once a helicopter followed me after I held up a post office at Gadds Hill. Luckily, I managed to lose him. On the second occasion, I was chased by a motor-cycle cop in Romford. He didn't stop me for the robbery I had just done; he pulled me up for overtaking cars on a zebra crossing. When he gestured me over I could hardly tell him I was speeding because I had just done an armed robbery so I told him to 'Fuck off'.

By now I had taken to using a motor-bike myself as they were easier than cars in traffic. So I opened up the throttle and ripped down the road with the motor-cycle cop in hot pursuit. When I looked behind me the cop was still chasing me. I knew I couldn't get away – I only had a 250 Honda – so I slowed down again and fired my gun over his head and off I went. Unfortunately, on that episode I dropped a wig so when I was eventually arrested they tied me with that one.

I knew then I had to get myself a more powerful bike, so I invested in a big red Kawasaki GPZ. I thought the bastards would never catch me on that.

Like I say things were getting too hot in Brentwood, so I decided to move my operations down to the coast.

My parents had retired to a little seaside village called Frinton. I had stayed down there on my summer holidays a few times, so I knew the area well. I remembered that there was also a village, not far away from Frinton, a place called Walton on the Naze, a busy little place quite popular with holiday makers. And I remembered that Frinton and Walton on the Naze both had post offices. I took a drive down to see my mother and to look at the possibility of robbing both shops. I couldn't believe my luck. They were perfect, only 20 minutes away from each other. This double job would set me straight and it would definitely be my last.

The date was 24 August 1984, three days before my thirty-fourth birthday. I had been doing armed robberies now for exactly two years.

I prepared all my usual disguises and plotted my escape route. The only problem I could see was where to stash the money after I did the first robbery and while I was doing the second? I only had a saddle bag on my motorbike and I kept my gun in that. So where the hell was I going to put it? Hopefully it would be a big bag of money. I deliberated over this for quite a while. Then I came up with an idea. I would do the first robbery, hide the money somewhere *en route*, do the second robbery, go to my mother's for tea, wait for a while, then pick up my hidden loot. I drove the route to and from the two post offices 50 times, scouring the countryside for a suitable hiding place. Eventually, I found a spot by a small bridge. It had a ditch underneath filled with rubbish. It was a perfect hiding place.

It was a beautiful hot August day. I waited until 4 p.m. before pulling on my jeans, trainers and leather jacket. I rode over to the first post office at Walton on the Naze and parked my bike about 200 yards away. I kept thinking to myself that this double robbery would be my last. The palms of my hands were sweating as I put on my brown wig, and pulled the stocking mask down over my face.

Quickly, I hurried across the road and burst into Walton

Post Office. I did a double take. There was a crowd of holiday makers still in there, all wearing shorts and kiss-me-quick hats, eating ice-cream and looking at the naughty postcard display. For some reason it was a surprise but I didn't mind. I preferred a crowd. I had learned that the more people there were to threaten, the more quickly I was likely to get the money. I shouted at them: 'Get up against the wall and you won't get hurt!'

I pointed my gun at the stunned crowd and ordered the cashier to fill the Tesco carrier bag with money – "Just notes – large notes!'

I turned to look at the sunburned bunch of holiday makers cowering against the wall. I smiled at them and said, 'This will give you something interesting to write on your postcards.'

The cashier nervously handed over the bag stuffed full of money. I snatched the bag and rushed out, pulling my stocking mask off as I ran. When I reached the small bridge where I had decided to hide the money, I looked around. Everything was quiet. Good! The place was deserted. I slid down the grassy bank clutching the bag. It felt as if there was quite a lot of money inside.

I wanted to stop and count it but I didn't have time. I had to get to Frinton and my next robbery.

There was a lot of rubbish in the ditch, and I had to push an old Tesco shopping trolley that had been dumped there out of the way. I concealed the bag as best I could. I was so wrapped up in my thoughts and what I was doing that I didn't notice a local lady driving past. Later, in court, she said she saw my bike parked by the bridge and wondered what I was doing in the ditch. She had thought I was dumping kittens in a black plastic sack and, being an animal lover, she was appalled.

She drove straight into Walton, where I had just done the robbery and told the police she had seen a man on a red motorbike dumping a black sack in a ditch. If only the nosy cow had gone the other way. The police wasted no time and made straight for the bridge. Of course, I didn't know that all this was going on – I was already on my way to Frinton and my next robbery.

I parked my bike by the church and walked into Frinton Post Office just on 5 p.m. There was only one little old lady left in the place. She was cashing her pension and chatting away to the cashier about the weather and, like lots of old ladies that you normally get stuck behind in the post office queue, she was completely unaware of what was going on behind her. I pointed my sawn-off shotgun at the cashier and shouted: 'Give me the money!'

He was cool. He was having none of it and politely told me to 'Fuck off!'

I was shocked by his reaction and pointed the gun at the old lady. 'You don't want this old lady to get hurt do you? Now, give me the fucking money – PLEASE!'

'Fuck off!' he snapped and pressed the alarm bell.

I realised then that I wasn't going to get a penny off him and I started to panic. As I turned to walk out, a lanky, spotty youth was walking in. He was only about 18 years old and very fit. Of course, when he saw me in my stocking mask

holding a gun and heard the alarm bells ringing, he decided
to be a hero and chase me. I ran down the alleyway adjacent
to the post office with the lanky youth hot on my heels. He
could run fast, bloody fast. It was like being chased by
Sebastian Coe.

Halfway down the alley, I stopped and screamed at him
to: 'Fuck off!'

I carried on running as fast as I could. When I turned to
look again he was still chasing me. I couldn't believe it. I
stopped and pointed my gun at him: 'This is your second
warning. Next time your foot comes off!'

I had long before decided that if I were ever chased I
would give a couple of verbal warnings. Then, if they still
took no notice, I'd fire the gun into the air or into the
ground, just to let them know it was a real gun. If they still
kept following me, then I would have no choice but to
blow their foot off. It's as simple as that. If it was a case of
me going to prison or them losing a foot, then so be it, they
would lose a foot.

After the second warning and me telling him I was
going to shoot his foot off, the lanky youth finally backed
off. Thank Christ!

I made my way back to my mother's as quick as I could.
She wasn't in but my niece was there in the driveway
working on her motorbike and sidecar. I rode my bike
straight into the open garage.

I had to think of a way of getting rid of the false number
plates without my niece becoming suspicious. I tried to act
normal and casually asked her how she was. Inside I felt sick

and my knees felt like jelly but I had to keep calm. 'What's up with your bike? Need any help?'

She didn't take much notice of me, she just went into this long speech about her pistons or crank shaft or something. I wasn't listening. All I could think of was getting those bloody number plates off my bike. I wandered back into the garage and quickly ripped them off and stuffed them behind an old dresser which was stored in the garage. I felt relieved. What a day! I needed a drink. I went into my mother's and poured myself a double vodka and gulped it down. I needed it. I slumped down in the big old comfortable armchair with the bottle in my hand. I needed to sit and gather my thoughts.

About an hour later, my niece came in, wiping her hands on a greasy bit of rag. She was moaning that she still had trouble with her bike.

I think the vodka must have given me a bit of courage because I offered to take it out for a test drive for her. I thought it would be the perfect opportunity to see if the coast was clear for me to pick up the hidden money. My niece had given up ever mending the bike herself and jumped at the chance of me helping out.

I drove slowly up and down the quiet road. Everything looked OK. Nobody was around so I got a little more daring and drove to the little bridge where I had stashed the money. As I got within about 50 yards of the bridge I started to slow down. Before I had time even to think of making an escape, I was surrounded. Police cars came from every direction. I knew I had no chance of getting away as the motorbike and sidecar only did 30 mph top whack. So I had no alternative but to front it out. I pulled the bike over to the grass verge and got off. The evening air was stifling and I went to open my leather jacket but the police screamed at me to put my hands on my head.

'What's the problem, officer? I've only opened my jacket. What's this all about?' All the time I was trying to act normal. They explained to me that there had been armed robberies in Walton and Frinton and they were looking for a man who escaped on a motorbike. I roared with laughter and pointed at my niece's pathetic-looking motorbike and sidecar. 'Do you really think that looks like a getaway bike? Its got a sidecar for Christ's sake!'

They agreed but said they had to be sure. The man they were looking for had a beard and, at that time, I had a beard too. They assured me they were only doing their job. I told them that I had just come from my mother's house, which was just down the road, and that I was road testing the bike for my niece. They said they believed me but they had to take me back to my mother's, just to make sure.

I got into the back of the police car, all the time hoping and praying that they didn't search me or they would have found some shotgun cartridges in my pocket. As we pulled up at my mother's, she was just going in the back door. As the police approached her, my big red Kawasaki bike was only 20 yards away. I felt sure they would see the reflected number plates but they didn't. They asked Mum if I was her son and how long I had been gone. Of course, Mum didn't know. Just then my niece walked in. She confirmed what I had said – I had only been gone for 15 minutes. That seemed to satisfy them. The two officers apologised for the inconvenience and insisted on giving me a lift back to my niece's bike.

When I got back home again, I needed a few more drinks to steady myself. By this time I was a nervous wreck. Mum cooked dinner but I couldn't eat a thing and only picked at it. All I wanted was a drink to keep me calm.

I sat on the step outside my mother's house with a beer, trying to find the courage to go and get the hidden money.

By eight-thirty I was well tipsy and felt sure by now the police would have given up and gone. I smiled to myself. I'd have one more drink, then I'd go and get all that lovely money that was just waiting for me. I don't know whether it was just the drink that was making me brave or perhaps I was just plain stupid. I pulled on my crash helmet, jumped on my Kawasaki and drove to the bridge. It was the worst mistake I ever made.

This time I pulled up about 200 yards away. It all seemed quiet enough. Because my niece had been in the garage earlier, I hadn't had a chance to take the loaded shotgun out of my saddlebag. Now I pulled it out and stuffed it into a black plastic bag. I thought I had better not leave it with the bike in case someone stole it.

Slowly, I made my way towards the bridge and the hidden money. The drink had made me so confident that all I could think about was getting my hands on that money.

There were a few cars parked on the verge but I didn't take any notice of them. I must have been drunk because I certainly didn't see the parked Ford Granada with four uniformed police officers sitting inside. I walked straight past them, in a world of my own.

I jumped over the little bridge and slid down the bank to the tree that I had marked so I'd be able to go straight to the money. There was lots of rubbish in the ditch and it looked different from earlier in the day, which confused me. I pulled off the trash that I had put on top of the bag. Great! it was still there. Eagerly, I tore the bag open but, to my horror, it was full with old newspapers. I must have the wrong bag. Frantically, I scoured around, looking for another black sack but I couldn't find one. I came out of the bushes on to the road to check if I had the right spot. Yes, I was in the right place but where was my money?

Of course, although I didn't know it, the woods were crawling with Old Bill. I started lifting up old mattresses and tyres searching for the money but I couldn't find it. In frustration, I shouted, 'Bugger it!' I had spent three days planning this double robbery, all that bloody hassle and some snotty nosed kids must have found my money and nicked it. 'What a bloody liberty!'

I must have been on another planet because it never occurred to me that maybe the police might have found it. I was deep in thought as I came out of the bushes and started to make my way back to my bike. I was mumbling to myself, 'Bloody kids!' I could have kicked myself. I'd had that money in my hands. If only I hadn't been greedy and tried to do the second robbery. Now I had nothing. If only … If only…

I walked past the Ford Granada again, completely

unaware that the four officers had got out of the car and formed a line behind me.

Three of them had .38 standard police revolvers, and were holding them in the double-handed position, aiming at me. The fourth had a double-barrelled shotgun and was holding it at his waist pointing at me. One of them shouted, 'Stop! We're armed police!'

I heard someone shouting but I was still in a dream world. I still thought it was kids, probably the little bastards who nicked my money. I didn't listen to what they were shouting, I just thought they were having a good time. After what seemed like ages, I heard it again, 'Stop! Police!'

Then it dawned on me that they were the police and they were shouting at me. I froze. For a few seconds I was stunned. My God what could I do? My motorbike was about 50 yards away, maybe I could make a dash for it. I turned my head and glanced over my left shoulder. By now it was 9.30 at night and it was starting to get dark. With the trees behind him I could only make out one copper. My mind was racing. If I fired a warning shot into the ground, maybe it would scare him off …

If only I had turned my head a little further round, then I would have seen the other three coppers standing to his right. But I didn't.

I had to make a split-second decision. My only option was to fire the warning shot, then make a dash for my bike. It was like it was all happening in slow motion. I started to run. My hand tightened around the bag containing the shotgun. As I started running, I turned and swung the gun up on to my left hip and aimed for the road in front of the copper. In an instant I had squeezed the trigger and for some reason both barrels went off. The bang was deafening and the kick from the 12-bore nearly blew the gun out of my hand.

From the moment I heard that deafening bang, I don't remember anything. I must have blacked out for a couple of minutes.

The next time I opened my eyes I was lying face down on the ground. I couldn't work it out. What was I doing lying in the road? I pushed my hands out in front of me and tried to pick myself up but I couldn't move my legs. I couldn't understand it. As I tried to push myself up I felt a searing pain in my back. I screamed out and total panic washed over me. I tried to wiggle like a caterpillar, thinking, 'What the hell's the matter with me?'

I must have blacked out again. Slowly, I opened my eyes. This time I was lying on my back looking down the barrels of about 12 guns. But I didn't care.

I was totally engulfed by the pain in my back. It felt as if my legs were twisted up my back. Instantly, I realised I had been shot. I screamed at the police to get me an ambulance. I winced, my eyes too scared to look down. When I did I could see I was lying in a pool of blood which was pumping from gaping holes in my hand, shoulder, leg and back. I screamed out, 'For God's sake, help me!' But nobody moved. The police just stood there aiming their guns at my head.

I saw the ambulance arrive and was shocked to see it go

straight past me. I tried to wriggle up and call out, 'I'm over here. I'm over here!'

But it didn't come to me. It went on about 30 yards away. That's when I became aware that someone else had been shot.

'Help me, help me, somebody help me. Straighten my legs! Please straighten my legs!' I pleaded with them to help.

But all they would say was, 'What's your name? Where do you live?'

Eventually I was bundled into the back of a second ambulance. I screamed at the doctor to straighten my legs. The doctor turned out to be my mother's GP and he held my arm tight. 'Lay still, Colin – your legs are straight.' He must have given me an injection because I passed out . . .

I opened my eyes. Everything was hazy. I didn't recognise the room. Everything was a brilliant white. Where was I? Was I dead?

I heard a bleeping sound in my ear. I turned my head. There were machines and monitors stacked up by the bed. Slowly, I put my hand out to touch them but I couldn't. I was joined up to drips and bags of blood. I looked down. There were tubes going up my nose, tubes in my chest and tubes in my side. I couldn't breathe and I pulled at the mask covering my face and tried to sit up but I couldn't move. I have never been so scared. At the end of the bed stood three stone-faced police officers. 'Oh, look, the bastard's awake,' they sneered.

For a moment I couldn't take it all in. 'Where am I? Why can't I move?'

The three coppers didn't take any notice. They sat down and carried on playing cards. I shouted again, 'Why can't I move?' One of the nurses must have heard me calling and came bustling into my room. She fiddled with one of the monitors and tapped one of the blood bags that was dripping slowly into my wrist.

'It's all right, Colin, you're in Colchester Hospital. You've been shot.' Her voice was so soft and reassuring.

'But why can't I move, nurse?'

Even with the voice of an angel, she couldn't soften what she had to tell me. 'One of the bullets went through your spine. I'm sorry, Colin, you're paralysed.' Her words echoed in my ears. Paralysed!

I felt a rush over my whole body and it all came flooding back to me. The robbery, the shooting and that dreadful pain in my back.

Over the next three days, I would wake up in the morning thinking, 'God, what a nightmare.' Then I'd realise it wasn't a nightmare after all. The three policemen at the bottom of my bed never spoke to me. The only thing they did say was that I was a dirty slag and that I had shot one of their colleagues, a PC Brian Bishop, and that he was in hospital, critically ill.

On 27 August 1983, my thirty-fourth birthday, a plain clothes copper came into the small room. His face was ashen. He stared at me with hatred in his eyes and said, 'They've just switched the life support machine off. PC Bishop's dead. It should be you, you bastard!'

From that moment on I was a cop killer and I couldn't

in my wildest dreams have imagined what lay in store for me.

Over the next month I was guarded day and night by the police from the station where PC Bishop had worked. Every one of the officers wanted to avenge their mate's death and there wasn't a thing I could do about it. I couldn't move or defend myself. I was completely at their mercy.

At first, it was small things like moving my water jug so I couldn't reach it or cutting the cord to the light switch so I couldn't turn my light off. I found it difficult to sleep anyway but they would play cards all night. I'll never forget it. They played crib and all night I would hear them calling – 15-2, 15-4, 15-6. It was driving me mad. They kept on and on until in the end I couldn't take any more. I leaned over and peered at the little clock on the bedside cabinet. It was 2 am. I snapped. 'Please, please keep the noise down – I've got to get some sleep'.

A young, fresh-faced copper slowly put his cards down on the table and pushed his chair back, scraping it across the shiny, polished floor. 'Keep the noise down! You cheeky bastard!'

I knew he was going to do something. I could see the hatred in his eyes.

'I've got a good mind to turn your oxygen bottle off. See how you like that!' Slowly, he turned the wheel on the oxygen cylinder and the hissing sound up my nose stopped. I was so scared. I stared at him in disbelief as I gasped for the last breath of air. As I neared unconsciousness, all I could hear was the three coppers laughing.

I was in hospital for six months until I was well enough to go on trial for murder. I was pushed into court in a wheelchair. In his summing up, the judge said that he would have recommended that I serve 20 years but my injuries were an added punishment so he would not give me a recommended sentence, only a life sentence. Only a life sentence!

Eleven years on, I really believe it would have been kinder to hang me rather than make me endure the existence of a disabled man in prison. On that day in court I was in a state of shock but I naively thought I'd be sent to a special prison, a prison for people with special needs. However, after a short stay in a prison hospital, my wheelchair and I were taken to Parkhurst Prison on the Isle of Wight. There, as in every prison I've been in since, there simply are no facilities for the disabled. They don't just take away your liberty – they take away every scrap of human dignity; they humiliate you, sometimes quite literally leaving you to lie in your own excrement.

I killed PC Brian Bishop and I don't expect your sympathy for that. But does it console you that, in doing so, I sentenced myself to a living death?

Charlie
Smith

Killers

'**T**here's a stiff in my cell. I don't know why I did it. He hadn't done anything to me . . .' The screws at Wormwood Scrubs rushed into the cell. There, dead in his bunk, was the lifeless body of 20-year-old car thief Paul Lehair. Psychopathic murderer, Charlie Smith, aged 20, had warned prison staff of his 'murderous ideas'. Charlie was already serving a minimum sentence of 20 years for stabbing and beating a drunken man to death in an Oxford park.

The facts are stark and disturbing. Charlie had been a wayward child and was boarded at a variety of schools for maladjusted children.

On 30 March 1977, he absconded from Borstal and killed the drunken stranger. He gave various reasons for this offence, including response to homosexual threat and robbery but the true motive has remained a mystery.

Once in prison, he attacked staff, one of whom he stabbed with a fork. By the time he reached the Scrubs he was so violent that a prison officer said that, one day, unless watched carefully, he would kill again. While in custody he had also abused himself by piercing his flesh with needles, had cut his arms with a razor and had tried to commit suicide by hanging himself.

Paul Lehair was just starting a six-month jail term when he found himself sharing a cell with Charlie. Smith complained to fellow prisoners that Lehair was 'dirty and did not wash' and asked staff to remove him from his cell. Arrangements were made to move Lehair the following day. However, before they did so, at midnight on Saturday 23 June 1979, a prisoner in a nearby cell heard a yell and a choking noise. The croaking sound made him uneasy but he told himself it was nothing to worry about and went back to sleep.

Charlie said:

> *I woke up in the middle of the night and saw him standing at the bottom of the bed. I thought it was my mother and I got up and attacked him. I tore the sleeve from his shirt and strangled him.*
>
> *The geezer was only serving six months. He did nothing to me. I did it — I'm very sorry.*

At the Old Bailey, Charlie Smith pleaded not guilty to

murder but guilty to manslaughter on the grounds of diminished responsibility. He was sent to Broadmoor without limit of time.

Fifteen years later he met and married my sister Maggie. With help from staff at Broadmoor and from Maggie, he has tried to come to terms with the horrific crimes he committed when he was a teenager. For the first time in his life he had somebody whom he loved – and who loved him.

In this chapter Charlie talks openly about the mental illness that led him to kill two innocent people …

★   ★   ★

Childhood days are meant to be something a person can look back on and remember – the happy, carefree days of innocence. But my childhood was a far cry from that. I have no happy, or even fond, memories of my childhood at all. My memories are terrifying.

I was born on 13 March 1959, in a prison. I only spent weeks with my natural mother. I was taken away and eventually adopted. The first eight years of my life were a complete misery. I had no normal family life and when I was bad, which was often, I was punished which I didn't always think I deserved. I was just like any other eight-year-old boy, a bit cheeky and a bit naughty.

Sometimes there were rows between my adoptive parents, which frightened me and made me feel guilty and unwanted. Maybe the rows were my fault, who knows?

Well, that's how I saw it. I really didn't understand what I had done wrong. I was all mixed up and only now do I realise that my childhood didn't help me very much.

My adoptive parents decided to adopt a little girl. I was taken along to collect my adoptive sister and I can still remember thinking, at the time, that maybe now things would get better. I was wrong. Nothing changed and, by now, as young as I was, I started to realise that I was on my own.

By the time I reached junior school age, instead of going to school, I was more likely to be found wandering around the streets on my own or playing on pinball machines in some arcade in town. I had to grow up quick to survive and, in doing so, I lost all my childhood. At the age of eight I was more streetwise than some kids twice my age. When I was at school, I was always in some kind of trouble or another. I had no interest whatsoever in education, something I later regretted. If something went wrong for me in the classroom, I would purposely shout and swear at the teacher until they had no alternative but to send me out of the room. This suited me because I could then go straight to the staff cloakroom and steal the teachers' money from their coat pockets and lockers. Even at break times I was always in trouble, mainly for fighting, and in the end I became pretty handy with my fists.

The only time I ever wanted to go to school was for the swimming lessons. I won all the distance certificates up to five miles, also the bronze, silver and gold for life saving. Swimming was something I enjoyed and still do.

Trouble used to follow me around and, in the end, I was

expelled from school. What happened was this. I was in an art class. I liked painting and I was quite good at it too. I was putting the final touches to a painting that I had done when, for no reason, this kid purposely threw a pot of water over it. I went mad. I lost my temper and tried to stab the kid with a pair of scissors. The teacher pulled me off and, luckily, the kid wasn't hurt. I don't exactly remember much about what happened. I was in a sort of daze. All I know is I was expelled about a week later.

By the tender age of eight I was already seeing a child psychiatrist and, after this incident in the classroom, social workers took over and moved me about like an old parcel.

First, they sent me to a special unit to be assessed. It was called Campion School and it was in Borehamwood. It was a real soft touch there; all I ever did was make plastic Airfix models. Next I was moved to an approved school called Hailey Hall in Hoddersdon. By this time it was 1970 and I was ten years old with a 'rebel streak' in me a mile wide.

Hailey Hall was a modern building set in acres of woodland. It had its own swimming pool too, which pleased me and, after school was over, I would go swimming or walk into the nearby town and wander around. I only had one friend at Hailey Hall. His name was Brian and we used to run away together, catch a train to Euston Station and make our way to Millwall Football Ground. We were always scrapping with the away supporters. Brian was expelled from Hailey Hall, I can't remember what for, but, later on in life, I met him again in Wormwood Scrubs Prison, where we were both serving life for murder.

While I was in Hailey Hall, I was arrested for the first time. It was nothing too serious; I was drunk and disorderly. I was only a kid and the copper who arrested me didn't give it a thought that I had been smoking dope as well. I appeared at Barnet Juvenile Court and was fined £15. By this time I was well into housebreaking and nicking cars. I would sneak off school and go thieving. In April 1972, I was again charged with burglary and robbery and was finally removed from Hailey Hall. I had been there two years.

I was taken to a more secure place to await my trial. When I appeared in court on 11 May 1972, they placed me on a care order until I was 18 years old. By this time my total disregard for authority was well established. I had no family, no friends. I was all alone. It was the beginning of a downward spiral that I had no control over.

I was taken to a remand centre for juvenile delinquents called Thornbury House in Kiddington, Oxfordshire. I was supposed to stay there while the teachers and social workers decided what to do with me but I was having none of that so I ran off to Great Yarmouth. It was pouring with rain, I was soaked to the skin and I just wandered around aimlessly until I noticed some Hell's Angels outside a cafe. I decided I wanted to join them so I took a deep breath and went into the cafe. I figured that if they didn't like me I would soon know about it and I'd probably end up in hospital.

I went up to the counter and ordered a cup of tea and then sat down in the corner. They seemed to be amused by the scruffy little urchin smoking a joint. I was 12 years old at the time. The president of the chapter must have felt sorry for me because he bought me a big breakfast and told me to eat up.

When they left, I went with them and we went to an old rundown squat on the outskirts of town. There were about 15 of us in all. They treated me quite well. After about three weeks, the Hell's Angels were involved in a running street battle with some skinheads, which lasted about two hours. There were police everywhere and one of the Angels suggested I leave a bit quick or I would be nicked with the rest of them. I was sad to leave them. I enjoyed my time with the Angels, but it was only a matter of time before I was caught and returned to Thornbury House.

That didn't bother me. Being in one institution was much the same as any other and Thornbury House wasn't too bad; the sports facilities were quite good there. I could play football and I also got loosely involved in karate and reached a green belt. But after a while I got fed up even with that and I was starting to feel restless again.

It was 1972 and I wanted desperately to go back to London so, in the middle of the night, I climbed out of the window, shinned down the drainpipe and took off. A few miles down the lane I came across a golf club that had been locked up for the night. I broke in through a window, stole £50 and caught a train to London.

I arrived at Paddington Station early in the morning. I was cold, hungry and all alone. I went straight to a cafe and ordered myself a breakfast, then I headed up west. Big mistake! No sooner had I arrived at my old stamping ground when the police who, by now, knew me quite well, picked me up straightaway. They decided to put me in a place called Sparrows Hearn, an assessment centre just outside Watford. There, they tried to educate me but all that education trip got on my nerves. I could read, write, fuck and fight, that was good enough for me. I figured that was all I needed to know.

I made various escapes from Sparrows Hearn. On one occasion I met a couple of girls who were on the game and I lived with them for a while. They were great fun to be with and they really opened my eyes to crime, also to the best ways to earn a few quid. Once again, I was caught for burglary, fraud and deception and, on 31 August 1973, I was found guilty at Barnet Juvenile Court and sentenced to three months in one of Her Majesty's detention centres.

It didn't bother me though. 'Ninety-two-days,' I thought. I had just finished working it out when the door burst open and three burly police officers came in and handcuffed me. They bundled me into a waiting police van and took me to Whatton Detention Centre in Nottingham – a bloody long way from London. On my arrival at the detention centre, the police handed me over to the screws as if I was a parcel for delivery.

The big, bolshy screw on reception asked me if I smoked. 'Yes,' I answered. He asked me again if I smoked, again I said, 'Yes.' Crack! He punched me so hard on the side of my head that I saw stars. He told me that all officers are called 'sir' and not to forget it. Detention centres were then what was commonly known as the short, sharp, shock treatment.

It was hard work; no more lazing about making plastic models. The day started at six o'clock in the morning when every inmate was tipped out of bed and ordered to wash. There was no such thing as hot water. All our bedding and clothes had to be folded military-style and if the screws didn't think it was good enough they would throw it all over the place and make us do it again. Every inmate had to be washed and shaved by 6.15 a.m., then it was out on the exercise field until 7 a.m.

After breakfast we would have to scrub the floors on our hands and knees till you could see your face in them. We did that until 10 a.m. From 10 a.m. until dinner time, we would be in the gym doing circuit and weight training. It wasn't the physical side of it that bothered me. I quite liked that side of it. But I hated the screws, their attitude and their sheer brutality.

After two weeks, because of what they called 'anti-social behaviour', I was put to work on the hole-digging party. This meant digging a big hole in the ground one day and then filling it in the next! The same mindless, pointless routine, day in, day out, nothing changed – change was, after all, against the rules.

One day I was in the dining hall with a friend of mine when, suddenly, a screw came over and punched my friend hard in his ear because we were talking. His ear started to bleed. Now this really annoyed me and some of the other inmates, so I organised a riot for tea time. After we finished eating, I started to bang my metal tray on the table. Soon, everyone was doing the same and the noise was deafening.

The screws knew something was about to erupt so they ran out and locked us all in the dining hall. After about an hour, the governor came and said we had made out point and we were to give it up or we would lose our remission. Ninety per cent of the rioters gave up and returned to their cells, leaving me and about four others to go it alone. The screws wasted no time. They rushed in and kicked us all the way to the punishment cells. Once the screws got me in that cell they beat me black and blue, then they held me down and injected me with a drug called Largactil which, throughout the prison system, is called a 'chemical cosh'.

I got another three months for that little episode but, more importantly, it made me realise that you can't beat the system. They can do whatever they want to you and you can't do a damned thing about it. You are completely at their mercy. They always win.

Eventually my release date came and I was collected from the detention centre by my social worker, only to be taken back to an approved school. But I had other ideas. As the car pulled up at the traffic lights, I jumped out and took off.

I went to Hampstead Heath and joined the fair. No one asked any questions and I loved the life. It was brilliant. For the first time in my life I was happy. The work was hard – putting up and taking down the rides, lugging all that equipment about, but I loved the responsibility that went with it. We moved all around the country and occasionally stopped off at some of the places that I was on the run from so I had to be careful. I was always looking over my shoulder.

In the summer of 1973, we were at a place called Abingdon in Oxfordshire. I was taking a bit of a chance because I had escaped from Hunterscombe Borstal which was only a few miles away. I had finished all my work early and decided to go fishing in the nearby river.

As I was making my way down to the river bank I noticed a little girl thrashing about in the river. I ripped my jacket off, dived in and pulled the little girl to safety. She was only four years old. She had been playing too close to the riverbank when she had slipped and fallen. The current was very strong and she was soon carried away.

Her parents were ecstatic that I had saved their little girl and that night they came to the fair. Her father told me that he had reported my actions to the police and also the newspapers as he thought I deserved a reward. 'Oh no,' I thought, 'not the police!' I made my excuses and was soon on my toes again.

This time I went to join a circus – The European Circus at Ilfracombe in Devon. It was brilliant. I loved animals, still do. While I was with them I saw a tiger give birth. She had three little cubs. The tiger would only allow me and my boss to go anywhere near her young cubs. My job was to feed and exercise the horses, tigers and two huge elephants at a place called Waltham Abbey. I used to walk the elephants into a river and scrub them down with a yard brush. It there wasn't a river close by, then I'd use a bucket and hose.

Working at the circus was very hard. I started work at four o'clock in the morning and I didn't finish until late in the evening. My job also involved putting up and pulling down the big top which was very tiring, especially when it was raining.

While I was with the circus I used to mess around on the trapeze during my spare time and eventually the boss offered me a sort of apprenticeship in Germany but only if I was prepared to give myself up to the authorities and get my punishment over and done with once and for all. But I was too full of myself. I didn't want to give up my spell of freedom. Maybe if I had listened to him, things might have turned out differently. Who knows? So I left the circus and returned to the West End of London.

The West End is a lonely place. You've got to be tough to survive there alone. There are all sorts of shady people around: pimps, whores, drug addicts, dossers and, of course, there are tourists. It's so easy to get sucked into the more seedy life of the West End. I soon got to know a few of the girls who were on the game and it wasn't long before I was earning a good living.

One of the tricks I would use to get money was to stand outside a block of flats with a card stuck on the wall saying: 'Model 2nd floor'. I'd then wait for a punter to come along and I'd sell him the key to the flat for £10. As soon as the punter made his way up the stairs I'd pull the card off the wall and get lost in the crowd.

I had a lot of little scams like that. By this time I was addicted to cocaine and I did anything to get my drugs. In that world, one day you'd have lots of money, living it up in posh hotels, the next day you'd be down and out at Charing Cross Station waiting for the soup kitchen to arrive. But I always seemed to find enough money for a line of coke and I was never seen without a joint in my mouth. Before I knew it, my worsening drug habit had taken over my life. I'd spend my whole day ducking and diving, stealing money for a fix. By night I was out of my head. Sometimes I would try to get myself together. Once, about a week before Christmas, I decided to take some presents home to my adoptive parents. I don't know if it was because it was Christmas, the season of goodwill, or what, but for some reason I thought that maybe, just maybe, they would be pleased to see me. I hadn't even reached the front door when they told me to get lost. I went there with all the best intentions, but I never went again and I've not seen them since.

Back up the West End, I had become totally mercenary about getting money to feed my drug habit. I broke into a garage and stole £500. I knew this money wouldn't last five minutes but I really didn't want to spunk it. You could do £500 on dope in no time at all and I wanted to put the money to some use.

I was sitting in a cafe in Victoria staring aimlessly out of the window, not thinking about much at all, when I noticed a large billboard opposite advertising a classic old film on the Foreign Legion called Ten Tall Men, starring Burt Lancaster. I studied the black and white billboard carefully then thought, 'Why not? What have I got to lose?'

Joining the Foreign Legion could be the fresh start I needed. So, on the spur of the moment, I caught a train to Dover and bought a ticket to Ostend. I changed all my money into French francs, only to discover that Ostend was in Belgium and not in France. However, I had made up my mind and was determined to go to France and join the Foreign Legion so now I had to catch a night train to Lyons. The train wasn't due until four o'clock in the morning, so I curled up on the seat and fell fast asleep, dreaming about my forthcoming adventure. As the train pulled into the station, it was pouring down with rain. In the cold light of day I remember thinking that maybe this wasn't such a good idea after all. I didn't really know where to start and I couldn't speak a word of French but, eventually, I was pointed in the right direction and found myself standing outside the recruiting office.

I was a bit apprehensive about going in and, after waiting an hour, I decided to leave but no sooner had I reached the door when the recruiting sergeant marched in. He was a large man, upright and expressionless, and there was no turning back now. He told me to strip for a medical examination. Then the army doctor came in and he looked like he had had a heavy night. I could smell the alcohol on his breath. After the examination, he abruptly told the sergeant I was fit enough to die in Chad.

Chad, I was later to find out, was in Africa. They were in the midst of a guerrilla uprising and Legion forces were there to suppress it. I also learned that the motto of the Legion was: 'A man's past is nothing – he is always fit enough to die'. The first bit suited me fine – but the rest of it wasn't what I had in mind at all!

After my medical, I was given a pair of combat boots, army shirt and combat trousers, then led into another room. There they played a tape recording in English which said that I was now a soldier of the Foreign Legion and that I would stay a soldier for five years, the minimum term. I signed about six sets of papers then, for some reason, I was locked in a room with two other young soldiers who had been caught trying to desert. They were in a terrible state. It was obvious they had been badly beaten and they looked as if they hadn't eaten for days. Putting me in that room with them was, I supposed, intended to deter the would-be deserter.

Ten minutes later, I was interviewed by the Foreign Legion security – tough, no-nonsense sort of men. They asked me my name, age and why I wanted to join the Legion. I told them the truth, in that I was on the run from the police in London, but I lied about my age and told them I was 19 when, in fact, I was really only 15.

They seemed to believe me because, after the interview, I was put on a train with two officers and taken to the training fort at Marseilles. It took two days to get there but I felt great. I had done it! At last I was a Legionnaire!

My first duty as a Legionnaire was to be driven to a remote camp about 30 miles away from the fort. There was me and about 40 others, all in full battledress, and the idea was for us to march back to the fort. It's bad enough having to march 30 miles in a day, but with a 60-pound kitbag on your back it's even harder. We eventually got back to the fort in the early hours of the morning. I was totally knackered and I slumped on to the hard wooden bed and went straight to sleep.

KILLERS

I was on an 18-week training course, after which we would be posted to Algiers ready to support the other troops already stationed in Chad. In the weeks that followed, I learned how to break a man's neck in one sudden movement, how to disarm a knife attacker and everything there was to know about the Russian assault rifle, the AK47. We were taught the best places to plant magnetic mines on cars, tanks and troop carriers and unarmed combat was learned the hard way. The instructors were tough, hardened soldiers who threw us around like rag dolls.

I had been on my training course for about seven weeks when I was again interviewed by the security force. Somehow, they'd found out my real age. They said I had to leave. I was really upset and pleaded with them to let me stay. They wouldn't have it but at least they agreed to give me an hour before phoning the police.

Once outside the fort I had nowhere to go and the thought of returning to London and falling back into my old ways filled me with fear. For the last seven weeks I had been drug-free and I hadn't been in any trouble. Now I felt I was back to square one. I'd made the effort to get clean but it just wasn't worth it. I caught a train to Amsterdam and the first thing I did when I got there was to score some dope. I wandered around stoned out of my brain for five days before being arrested for attempted robbery.

I stayed in a Dutch prison while they sorted out the formalities to have me deported and eventually I was put on a ferry heading for Harwich. The British police were waiting for me and, as soon as the ferry landed, they arrested me and charged me with burglary and robbery. It was 19 September 1974, and at the time I had no idea that it was my last spell of legal freedom.

I stood in the dock of St Albans Crown Court and faced the judge. I had already spent five months on remand and now I was sentenced to two years in Borstal.

They took me away, bundled me into a green police van and drove to Wormwood Scrubs. It was my first taste of prison but I wasn't bothered. My whole life had been spent in some sort of institution. By the time we reached the Scrubs it was 8 p.m. and in the prison reception I was handed a 'Borstal boy' kit, which consisted of two pairs of jeans, two shirts, two sets of underwear, sheets and a pillow case. Goodbye to freedom! We were all escorted through the bleak old prison to B Wing, where we were given blankets, a plastic washing bowl and a water jug and then ordered to wait.

After a while I was called out by a big arrogant screw who promptly told me that from now on I was no longer a person, from now on I would be known as 931684. He then pushed me into a cell and slammed and locked the door. I'd already learned to hate screws in the detention centres and this pig was no exception.

I soon learned that being in a place like Wormwood Scrubs was very different to any other institution that I had ever been in. The life was tough, and you had to be too to survive. For a start, the boredom is enough to drive you mad. I was locked up for 23 hours a day with nothing to do, then let out for just one hour's exercise in the small courtyard.

The everyday sounds of the nick can sometimes make you feel you're going insane, with doors being kicked open or slammed shut, cons screaming, screws shouting and radios blaring and the smell of a prison is enough to make you vomit. I can only describe it as a mixture of fear, sweat and urine. Then there's the screeching cry of the starlings, sparrows and pigeons as they fly from the rafters in the roof. It seems daft to me why these birds choose to fly into a big cage. If I was a bird I would fly out, not in.

The screws themselves are enough to drive you nuts. They're all one and the same, a truncheon strap hanging out of the pocket, the slashed peak on the cap pulled down over the eyes, and the keys, which they swing from one hand to the other, on a long length of chain, which they think makes them look tough. Add the fat beer belly and a screw really is an unfortunate specimen of a human being. It was like entering a world of make believe and all these things were starting to get me down.

I could feel the anger and the hatred starting to build up inside. I started to blame my step parents, the screws, the system and just about everybody for the way my life had turned out.

It didn't help having nothing to do with my time except think for 23 hours a day and all I could think about was how my life was a total fuck up.

The only thing that breaks up the monotony of prison life is a visitor from the outside world. For a short time it's like being normal again, talking about normal things.

Getting news from the outside world is one of the most important things when you're away. But it's strange, when you've got a visit, you look forward to it for days before and by the time it finally arrives you think you've got a million questions to ask them. But, when you see them, after only 15 minutes you usually find you've run out of things to say. Then it's back to the world of reality: slamming doors, screaming prisoners and the loneliness of your cell.

Wormwood Scrubs prison was only an allocation centre for Borstal boys, thank God. The cells were filthy, there were armies of cockroaches marching across the floors and the food was diabolical. All in all, it was just one big garbage bin. I was only too pleased to see the back of the Scrubs and when I was eventually taken to Huntercombe Borstal I was relieved. It was so much better than the Scrubs. It was easier to escape from too! So it wasn't long before I was off again.

This time I escaped with a lad called Dave. He had some family problems to sort out and was desperate to get home. On the other hand, I just escaped for the hell of it. We went our separate ways when we hit London. I made my way to Chingford, to a friend named Terry. I had to get rid of my Borstal uniform and Terry fixed me up with some clothes and gave me some money for my fare back to the West End. As I left him, he pushed a five pound note into my hand. I thanked him and went on my way. I was glad to be on my own again.

I needed more money and, as soon as I was in town, I bought myself a knife. I then phoned a cab, booking it to go to Northampton. When the cab arrived, I jumped in the back. The driver was right friendly but after ten minutes I leaned forward, held my knife to his throat, and demanded all his money. He couldn't give it over quick enough. I felt a bit rotten as he was so nice, but I reckoned my need was greater than his. I told him to pull over. I grabbed the money and was off like a shot. Straight away, I hopped on to a bus to King's Cross. I booked into a hotel and when I got into the room I counted the money. There was just under three hundred pounds. Great! I showered, then slept.

Early the next morning I left the hotel and made my way to Hampstead Heath. My plan was to join the fair again and when I reached the heath I couldn't believe my luck as the fair was just being set up. I got a job straightaway. It took me a bit of time but soon I was set up with my own trailer. I had also met a girl named Sue. I was feeling right happy with myself.

Sue couldn't live with me but came to see me every day and followed the fair around. For the first time in my life, I was going straight. No drugs, no thieving. It felt good. Unfortunately, it wasn't to last.

The fair had just arrived at Bamton, Oxfordshire. Sue was waiting for me there. The fair was not opening until the next day so that evening we went for a drink in the local pub. We had not been there longer than half an hour when the Old Bill walked in. I just knew they were looking for me. God knows how they tracked me down, but they had. They arrested me and held me at the local nick. Sue came down to the cells to see me before they shipped me back to Borstal. She said she would write but I knew it was over. I was gutted.

Back in Borstal, I was put on punishment for a few days and lost four months' remission. I didn't care. I had lost my job, my home and my girlfriend. I had nothing else to lose.

I wasn't in the mood to be messed about by any of them and, after a few run-ins with the screws, I was transferred to Dover Borstal, a place on top of the cliffs, where there was no chance of escape. Most of the time, I was on punishment in solitary confinement after getting into constant confrontations with the screws but, as far as I was concerned, it was me against the whole fucking system. Looking back, I believe that being in solitary for six long months in Dover pushed my mental health to the limits.

Eventually, I was seen by the Borstal doctor. I remember overhearing one of the screws saying, 'That boy's mad.' So, typically, they moved their problem, i.e. me, on. I was transferred to Feltham Borstal but they, too, couldn't handle me and eventually they shipped me back to Wormwood Scrubs.

By now I had done 18 months of my two-year sentence. No sooner had I arrived there than I was taken to see the governor and he informed me that I was to be released. I couldn't take it in. I didn't believe him. I knew I had lost all my remission. By this time I didn't trust anyone. I was totally paranoid about the system and I thought they were just trying to do my head in. I told the governor to get lost but he showed me a letter from the Home Office, confirming my release. Then I was over the moon. I was soon to be back on the streets. I couldn't wait!

As soon as I was released I made my way to my old

stamping ground of the West End. I didn't have anywhere to go and just wandered around until I bumped into one of the street girls I knew, who offered me a bed for a couple of nights.

For the next two weeks I was stoned out of my head 24 hours a day. At first it was brilliant but soon I began to feel very strange. Some days I would wake up not knowing where I was or how I got there. I started to think that people were after me and wanted to hurt me. I was angry and bitter. I knew I had to get away from the West End and the whole drug scene or I was going to end up back in trouble and back in solitary.

I'd heard that there was a fairground in Cirencester, Gloucestershire, so I packed my things and caught a National Express coach to see if I could get a job. The boss of the fair gave me a start working on the dodgems. It was OK but I wasn't feeling right. I was so mixed up in my mind, I still didn't trust anyone. I thought everyone and anyone was out to get me. All my life had been a struggle; I was 17 years old and nobody cared whether I lived or died.

I left the fair and started to travel about the country. Every town I hit I scored some dope. It didn't mater what it was, coke, heroin, anything, just to get out of my head and get me through the whole miserable day. All it did was make my paranoia worse.

It was a cold, dark, stormy night when I decided to catch a train back to London. I didn't have any money so I had to jump the trains.

By the time I reached Oxford I had missed the last train

to London. I was totally pissed off. I wandered around the station, kicking the chocolate machine, trying to get a free bar of chocolate out and then I noticed this man watching me.

I looked at him, then quickly looked away. He was a big man, about six feet tall, and built like a heavyweight boxer. I felt my heart racing. I looked back. Yes, he was still watching me. I didn't know what to do. I looked again and this time I stared straight at him. He gave a sideways glance then turned and walked away. I followed him. He went into a call box just outside the station. I felt sure he was talking about me. I moved closer to the call box to try to catch some of his conversation but I couldn't hear anything. He turned his back when he saw me. I knew then that he was talking about me. But who to? The police, maybe. Or maybe he was a policeman himself. I ran back to the station entrance and waited. I watched him come out of the call box and saw him make his way down the road.

I followed him nervously. He kept turning round, looking to see who was following him. I had to ask him who he was talking to in the phone box, I had to know. By the time I caught up with him we were in a park. It was dark and nobody was around. I grabbed his arm and said, 'Who was you talking to on the phone? You was talking about me, wasn't ya?'

He was calm: 'No I wasn't,' he said.

Then he pushed me away. I went berserk, punching him and kicking him until he fell to the ground. I turned around and started to make my way up the path, when, all of a sudden, he jumped up. As I turned to 'front him out', he grabbed me around the throat in a vice-like grip. I struggled and struggled, but he was too strong. I couldn't get him off. He was shouting and screaming at me and just wouldn't let go.

I don't know what happened to me; I totally lost control. While we were struggling, I pulled out my knife and began to stab him over and over again. First in the arms, just to make him let go of my throat, then in the legs. Eventually I had no choice; I stabbed him in the throat. As the knife went in, I felt his grip loosen. We were both covered in blood that was pumping from his wounds. He let go suddenly and slumped to his knees. My eyes felt as though they were bulging out of my head with the drugs I had taken.

Everything went quiet. I looked down at him, the knife still in my hand. I looked down at the body. I'm sure he was still alive. But I couldn't be sure.

My mind was racing so fast I couldn't think straight. I turned and started to run. I ran and ran until I couldn't run any more. I slumped against a wall out of breath and looked down at my blood-soaked hand still holding the knife. Was I dreaming? Did I just imagine it? Oh God, what had I done? I threw the knife away. What a terrible mess. I lit a cigarette and tried to get my head together. I knew the only thing I could do was get back to London. I would be safe there.

God knows how I got back to London but I did. I was living in a terrible nightmare. I kept thinking that maybe he wasn't dead. After all, he was alive when I left him. I tried to convince myself. I prayed he was alive. But in my heart I knew he was dead. I didn't know what to do. I had nowhere to run and nowhere to hide. All the years of fighting, all the unhappiness – I couldn't take any more. I didn't have a future. I was nothing.

Suddenly it all became clear to me. If I was to give myself up they would put me in prison forever. No more sleeping rough, no more drugs, no more fighting, no more nothing. At least I would get three square meals a day and be warm and have something consistent in my life.

My mind was totally confused. I decided to go to a Borstal that I had previously escaped from. God knows why. I walked into the reception and told the screw I wanted to see the governor immediately about a serious matter. He could see that I meant what I said. He unlocked the door and escorted me down a long corridor. It seemed to take forever. I can remember counting the lights on the ceiling and the number of doors we passed. When we arrived at the governor's office, the screw sat me down on the bench outside and I lit a fag. Under different circumstances, the screw would have told me to put the fag out but he never said a word.

When the governor arrived, he took me into his office and I told him the whole story. I was taken downstairs and put in a punishment cell. I was only there for about two minutes when the door opened and a screw came in with a chair. He'd been told to keep my mind occupied until the police arrived. He tried to talk to me but I was in such a state that I was in no mood for light conversation.

Eventually, I was taken back to Oxford and placed in a cell. Once again, the door was left open and a policeman stood in the doorway to make sure I didn't try to escape or commit suicide. I stayed in Oxford police station for about five days. They asked me a million questions. I answered what I could but by this time I was having a real bad come down from the drugs and I barely knew what was happening.

I remember appearing in court, being remanded, then shunted about the country to different prisons. Sometimes I was put in the hospital wing, other times I was put in the mainstream prison. In the end, I was taken to Leicester Prison and placed on Category A, high security risk.

I hadn't been there long when a so-called hard man came into my cell while I was shaving and demanded all my tobacco. I spun round quick and slashed him in the face with my razor. I was dragged down to the punishment cells and charged with assault and I stayed on punishment for 56 days.

My court case started on 7 October and lasted for three days. The clerk of the court told me to take the oath but I wouldn't and threw the oath card and the bible at the judge. When it came to sentencing, he gave me five years for GBH, 14 years for robbery with violence and life imprisonment for murder. I was 18 years old.

I was taken back to Leicester Prison to start my life sentence but I wasn't well. I got into all sorts of trouble and in the end I was taken back to the Scrubs.

I soon started to get the same feelings as I'd had when I killed the man in the park. Only this time I recognised that

I was ill. I told the prison doctor how I felt and he immediately moved me into a cell on my own. The next morning the screws put me back in my old cell. I pleaded with them. I told them I wasn't feeling well but they wouldn't listen.

That evening I smoked a joint and sat on my bed. I kept looking at my cell mate. He was about the same age as me, 18, and was serving three months for stealing cars. That's all I knew about him. We didn't talk much to each other and he didn't say anything to annoy me or give me any reason to hurt him. But all the things that had happened to me in my life came rushing back – how all the fault lay in my childhood. The more I looked at him, the more I imagined he was my adoptive mother. I felt all the anger and rage well up in me. The next thing I remember is waking up in the morning and seeing him lying in the corner of the cell; his tongue was hanging out and he was purple. I had strangled him. It must have been me, mustn't it? I picked his lifeless body up from the floor and laid him on his bunk. The screws unlocked the cell door. I didn't say a word, neither did they. I was charged again with murder and was sent to Broadmoor Hospital for the criminally insane with no limit of time.

Avril Gregory

Killers

A 16-year-old schoolboy was chatting to friends in the high street at Wombwell, near Barnsley. Minutes later, he staggered for 300 yards, then fell dying at the feet of a woman who knew him. Sandra Taylor, 34, said; 'I thought it was a drunk at first. Then I realised it was young Scott. I have known him since he was a kid. I asked him what was wrong. I could see then that there was blood everywhere. He was holding his right hand across his chest and the blood had covered his shirt, underneath his anorak.' She raced to a nearby club and two doormen rushed to his aid but the kiss of life failed to revive him. He died soon afterwards in Barnsley District Hospital.

Scott Beaumont was a keen footballer and a popular

member of the Angler's Rest football team. He lived in Hadfield Street, Wombwell. He had been due to leave the local high school in two weeks and hoped for a job as a garage fitter. A friend, Craig Taylor, spoke of how Scott had made an eerie prediction of his death. 'Out of the blue, he said he would hate to be dead and wondered what it would be like,' said Craig.

Nicola Mott, 16, Avril Gregory, 18, and two other young girls claimed that Scott had spoiled their holiday in Cleethorpes, Humberside, by calling them slags and taunting them. The teenage girls went hunting for him in a car driven by Kieron Wallbridge, 19. When they found him in a street near his home, Mott plunged a six-inch knife into his heart.

Mott and Gregory, of Hoyland, South Yorkshire and Beverley Snowden, 15, also of Hoyland, all denied murder in May 1992. Mott's sister Julie was also charged with murder but died in a road accident before the case came to court.

Mr Roger Keen QC said that although Mott had struck the deadly blow, the other girls had encouraged her and were jointly responsible for Scott's death. The jury acquitted Beverley Snowden and Kieron Wallbridge after nearly 12 hours' deliberation but Nicola and Avril were convicted by majority verdicts.

The judge told them: 'You are responsible for the death of a young man. There is only one order I can make in this case.'

The two girls clutched hands in the dock of Sheffield Crown Court and then wept in each others arms as Mr Justice Swinton Thomas ordered them to be detained during Her

Majesty's Pleasure. Mary Beaumont, mother of the victim, was in tears afterwards when she said, 'Scott is now at peace, but those two will never rest. It has been a terrible traumatic time for the whole family, but in the case of those two justice has been done.'

I was introduced to Avril Gregory by Linda Calvey, in Durham Prison. Linda has taken young Avril under her wing and Avril affectionately calls her 'Ma Barker'. Linda, Avril, another woman lifer and I sat in the small visiting hall drinking tea and chatting. We were swapping funny stories and screaming with laughter at different things, just as normal girls do when they get together. But these were not 'normal' girls. They were murderers – doing life. I asked Avril what happened. The mood suddenly became very serious. This is what she told me.

★   ★   ★

It was just another Friday night – Friday night and nowhere to go. I was in my room playing around with my hair in front of the mirror and listening to my favourite rave tape – loud. I heard my mum shout up the stairs, 'Avril, turn that racket down! Nicky's on the phone.'

I ran down the stairs. Mum shook her head and tutted as I took the receiver from her.

'Hi, Nicky,' I said, but all I could hear down the phone were sobs.

'He's going to get me, Avril, he's going to get me.'

I tried to calm her down. 'Who's going to get you?'

She said she had seen Scott Beaumont earlier in the day in the neighbouring village where Scott lived. They had had another argument and Scott had said that he was going to 'get' Nicola. He said that he, his girlfriend and a gang of 30 girls were going to bash her up.

The first thing I knew about any row was when Nicola came home from her holiday in Cleethorpes, Humberside. She said she had met and had a row with a lad called Scott Beaumont. He'd got the needle with her over something silly – to this day, I don't really know what it was all about. Things came to a head after Nicola and her 16-year-old sister Julie had a slanging match in the street with Scott. They'd slagged each other off, called each other names and said all the stupid childish things that any teenager might say. This must have really given Scott the hump because not long after he sent his girlfriend and a gang of girls to chase Nicola and her friend Beverley and threaten them.

When the girls came back from their holiday, they told me bits and bobs about the ongoing row, and I overheard snatches of conversations when they were talking about it, but I never really knew exactly what went off. To be honest, I wasn't very interested. It didn't concern me. I didn't go on the holiday with them, so it didn't involve me at all.

But when Nicky had seen Scott earlier that day, he threatened her, 'Be ready. We will be in Hoyland town tomorrow night at eight.'

Nicola was really frightened. She was convinced that he meant what he said and that Scott Beaumont was out to kill her. She kept saying, 'He's going to get me. He's going to kill me. I just know it.' She pleaded with me on the phone to help her, and asked if I would go with her the next night and stick up for her. She also asked me to get her 'something' . . .

Straightaway I knew what she meant – at the time my parents owned a small martial arts shop in the town. So, when she asked me to get her 'something', she obviously wanted me to get her something out of the shop.

The next day was Saturday 9 May 1992, and I was working all day in my parents' shop. I would be alone most of the day and thought that would be the perfect opportunity to get something for Nicola. At first I was hesitant. What if my parents found out? I had never taken anything from the shop before.

All that day Nicky was on my mind. She was so frightened. I had to help her, I had to get her something to protect herself with, but what? I really didn't know what to take. In the end, I settled for two knives. One was called a Tanto, a vicious-looking knife about six inches long with a straight blade. The other was a commando knife, seven inches long, with serrated edges on both sides. I don't know why I decided on those two, somehow they just looked right. I unlocked the glass cabinet and quickly stuffed them into my handbag.

Later that night Nicky phoned and said she would be around at seven along with her friend Bev and her sister Julie. She asked me if I had managed to get her anything from the shop and I told her about the two knives but I still wasn't sure if they were the right thing to get, maybe she didn't want a knife, maybe she wanted just a stick. I didn't know. So I told Nicky to go to my other friend's house on the way round and pick up a baton that I knew she kept. It was a baton just like the police use and I'd bought it for her as a prezzie after her boyfriend had left her. She was living in a bad neighbourhood; all kinds of creeps prowled around the place and she'd been frightened more than once. So I got her the baton out of my parents' shop. I told Nicky to stop off on her way round and collect it. I knew my friend wouldn't mind.

By seven the girls were at my house and we all went up to my bedroom. The other three were buzzing with excitement and said they'd got some 'things' too. We laid all our weapons out on my pink frilly bedspread. It looked like a bloody armoury. Altogether we had the two knives from the shop, the baton from my friend's house, a pickaxe handle and a crowbar. Eagerly, we shared out the weapons. Both the knives were in sheaths. I took the seven-inch, serrated knife and clipped it on my belt. Julie had the other knife, Bev had the crowbar and Nicky had the pickaxe handle.

We were all laughing and giggling, chatting away as girls do when they are all together. We were all posing, pushing each other out of the way at the mirror, doing our hair and using each other's lipsticks. Beverley and Julie were only 14 and were trying to make themselves look older. Nicky was 15 and, being the oldest, I was trying to advise them on hair and make-up and what was in fashion and what wasn't. I thought I knew it all, but what the hell did I know? I was only 17 myself!

I pulled on my Reebok trainers and my new black bubble

jacket and as we came bouncing down the stairs, trying to hide our weapons, I called out to Mum and told her I wouldn't be home that night as I was staying at my friend's house.

'OK, see you later, love,' she called.

Hoyland was our nearest town and the centre was only a ten-minute walk away. All the local kids from the neighbouring villages used to meet up at the local newsagents, on a bench outside. We arrived just before eight, and waited for Scott and the gang of girls. By about quarter to nine it was obvious he wasn't coming. I suppose in a way we were relieved he wasn't there.

A car drove up with a lad in it who Bev and Julie knew, called Kieron. They jumped out in the road and flagged him down. 'Give us a lift,' they squealed. 'Take us to the fair.'

A travelling funfair had set up in the nearby village of Wombwell earlier that week and we were all dying to go. Poor Kieron didn't have much choice really, because we had already bundled into the back of his car. There wasn't much for the kids in all the small villages to do, so we all looked forward to the fair. We thought that was our best bet – Scott would most probably be there.

We weren't looking for an argument with Scott but I suppose we wanted to show him that we weren't scared of him or the girls that he had set on Nicola and Beverley. The way we saw it was that after Scott's girlfriend and her gang had chased them, the row was more with them now and not Scott.

When we arrived at the fair it was buzzing. I love fairgrounds with their bright lights and loud music, the smell of fried onions and hot-dogs, the whirl of the dodgems.

We walked around the rides looking for Scott but couldn't find him. We found his little sister trying to win a goldfish at one of the sideshows. She told us that Scott was at home but he would be coming into town later. By this time we were caught up in the atmosphere of the fair and we weren't too bothered whether we found Scott or not.

We had a ride on the big wheel and the dodgems and forgot all about Scott and the row. When we were getting low on money we went and found Kieron and asked him to give us a lift home. We all bundled into Kieron's car and were chatting away. Kieron said, 'Which way home? Shall I take the short cut or shall I drive into town? Then we can get some chips!'

'Yeah! Let's get some chips.'

As we were driving through the high street, one of the girls spotted Scott. 'Stop! Stop! There he is, I'm sure it was him!'

Kieron drove to the end of the high street, then turned around. As we drove back up past the group of youngsters standing on the corner, we could see Scott, laughing and chatting away with his mates. It was him all right.

When he saw us he started to run a little way up the road. I don't suppose he wanted to be shown up by four screaming teenage girls in front of his mates. Kieron spun the car around and drove up a sidestreet. 'It's nothing to do with me,' he said. 'I'll wait here.' He lit a fag, pushed his new tape of chart music in the cassette player and settled back.

The four of us girls jumped out of the car and started to

walk down the street. Scott was at the other end with his three mates.

It was just like a scene out of a corny Western. All the shops were closed up for the night and most of the street lights were turned off. We carried on walking, past a cafe, past a newsagents. We all had our weapons. I still had the knife on my belt and Julie had the other knife, Bev had the crowbar and Nicky had the pickaxe handle. All of a sudden, Nicky stopped and said, 'I don't want this' and handed the pickaxe handle to her sister, Julie.

I don't know what made me do it, but I opened my coat and motioned to the knife in my belt and said to Nicky: 'Do you want this?'

She just nodded and whispered, 'Yes.'

Slowly, I pulled the knife out of the sheath that was still clipped to my belt and handed it to Nicky. I didn't realise at the time that that was the biggest mistake of my life.

Nicky walked on slightly ahead of the rest of us. When she reached Scott, they started arguing, shouting abuse at each other. I didn't see the knife. I didn't know if she had put it in her pocket, up her sleeve or what. Scott's three friends and the rest of us didn't say a word. We just all sort of stood back and let Nicky and Scott argue it out. After a while the argument seemed to be going around and around in circles; they were just shouting at each other.

I was getting a bit fed up listening to all the yelling, so I said the words that were to get me a life sentence: 'Go on, Nicola, don't let him see you're bluffing.' But, honestly, never for one moment had I meant for her to stab him. It never crossed my mind that she would even attempt it. She might not even have heard what I said — at least she didn't look at me or acknowledge me in any way.

It seemed like ages later that she pulled the knife out, but in reality it could only have been a matter of moments. They were still screaming at each other. All of a sudden I saw Nicky's arm go up, then shoot out. I couldn't see what she had done as I was standing directly behind her but I could see Scott clearly. I saw him clutch his chest and give out a gasp. There was a look of shock on his face. For a split second he glared at Nicky in disbelief. Then he turned in a flash and ran down the road.

For a moment I was stunned. Up until that point Scott had been winning the argument. I couldn't believe he was now running away. Running from four girls. What a wimp! I ran after him. As he reached the end of the street and turned the corner, I threw my arms in the air and shouted, 'That's one up to us!'

The next minute the rest of the girls were calling: 'Come on, Avril, let's go!'

When I got back to the car Nicky was in a terrible state. Julie said, 'Avril, she's stabbed him.'

I couldn't believe it! Nicky handed me the knife. I didn't even look at it. I just rammed it back into the sheath which was still clipped to my belt. Nicky must have been in a state of shock. She was shaking and crying and kept saying over and over, 'What if I've killed him? What if he's dead?'

All of us tried to calm her down, saying, 'No, you couldn't have hurt him, he had a thick coat on, you couldn't have got through all those clothes.' In trying to convince Nicky, I think the three of us convinced ourselves that he wasn't hurt and that he was all right.

Kieron never said a word, he just drove us back to Nicky and Julie's house. When we reached the house it was in darkness. Kieron pulled the car up outside and switched the engine off. Someone said, 'Let's look at the knife and see if there's any blood on it.'

I opened the car door so the interior light came on. Slowly I pulled the knife out of the sheath. As I did I could see blood smeared up the full length of the razor-sharp blade. Nicky screamed, 'Oh my God! No! No!'

I tried to reassure her and said, 'No, Nicky, it's all right. You must have just scratched him and as I put the knife back in the sheath the blood smeared up the blade. That's all, it's probably not as bad as it seems.'

I wanted to believe what I was saying but even as I said it the words seemed empty and hollow. I suppose in my own mind I was desperately looking for a logical excuse. I said, 'Don't worry, Nicky, you won't have hurt him.'

Beverley decided to go home. Kieron stayed in the car and waited for us. The three of us went inside the house to sort ourselves out.

Once inside, Nicky burst into floods of tears and ran upstairs. Julie collected the stick and the crowbar and put them in the cupboard under the stairs. I still had the knife in my hand and said to Julie, 'What shall I do with this?' In the light of the hallway I could see that there was much more blood on the knife than I'd thought. I said, 'Julie what can I do?'

'I know!' she said, 'Wash it!'

I ran into the kitchen and plunged the knife under the running tap to wash the blood off. My hands were shaking. Julie threw me a pink and white towel that had been folded up on top of the washing machine. I wiped the blade and put it back in the sheath, then stuffed it in my coat pocket, along with the other one. I was going to put them back in my parents' shop the very next chance I had.

At that moment Nicky came down the stairs. She looked awful. None of us knew what to do next. Then someone said, 'Let's get Kieron to take us for a drink.'

We needed an alibi and we thought that if we were seen in a crowded place then we would be all right. We all got back into Kieron's car and he took us to our local pub. We normally went to that particular pub on a Saturday night, so it wasn't unusual for us to walk in. It may have been normal any other night but tonight was different. As we walked in the pub, I felt as if we stood out like a sore thumb. I felt like everyone was looking at us.

Nicky and Julie got a table and sat down. I walked up to the bar and ordered three cokes. Then I heard a voice call out: 'Avril! Avril! over here!' I nearly jumped out of my skin. I turned and saw my mum's smiling face. She was waving her arms so I could see her across the crowded bar.

I was so relieved to see her and went over. She was sitting with my dad and some of their friends. It was a strange feeling but I felt safe sitting with them. I didn't want to go back to my friends' table. I looked over at Nicky and Julie sitting in the corner where I had left them. They looked like frightened little rabbits. I couldn't leave them to it. I had to go back to them. I made my excuses to my parents and told them I wouldn't be coming home that night. They gave me a kiss and said, 'OK, love!'

I walked back to my friends and all the time I was trying to act normal. When I reached the table, Nicky was crying. I snapped at her, telling her to shut up and not to bring attention to us. It was no good, she was inconsolable. We drank our drinks and left the pub. We decided to go back to their house. Nicky ran straight upstairs and slammed her bedroom door. Julie got the baton out of the cupboard under the stairs and we decided it would be a good idea if we took it back round to my friend's house. We knocked on the door and she let us in and made us a cup of coffee. I nervously handed her the baton. She said thanks and threw it in a drawer, not knowing the awful truth about what had happened.

Her boyfriend was out for the night so us three girls sat round the fire drinking coffee and chatting. In the end Julie decided to go home but my friend said I could stay so we went upstairs to bed. I didn't want to be on my own that night and I asked her if I could sleep in the same bed as her. She didn't think anything of it; she just thought I was scared of the prowlers that she had told me about.

We snuggled down in the bed and the next thing I remember is being woken up suddenly by loud banging on the door. I knew it couldn't be my friend's boyfriend, Nigel, because I had heard him come in earlier.

All of a sudden the bedroom door burst open. Nigel came

rushing into the room and said, 'Avril, wake up. There's someone here to see you. It's the police!'

Straightaway, I knew the lad was dead. I don't know why, call it a gut feeling, but as soon as Nigel said the police were there, I knew.

A policeman came upstairs and stood in the doorway and asked me if I had been in Wombwell town that night. I said, 'No.'

He said, 'We know you were there, Avril. We've arrested your friends. The incident that took place tonight has resulted in the death of a boy.' Even though I had a feeling he was dead, the words still stung my ears. 'Come on,' he said, 'get dressed. You're under arrest!'

They searched my friend's house and found the baton. They also searched through my clothes and found the two knives. One of the police officers spoke into his radio and, while I got dressed, four CID officers came for me. They handcuffed me, put me in the back of a police car and drove me to the nearby police station. I was put in a cell and the duty officer asked me if I wanted a solicitor. I said, 'Yes.' They slammed the cell door shut. I looked around at the graffiti on the walls of the cold, smelly cell and lay down on the bed. I pulled the grey, itchy blanket up over me and fell fast asleep. I think it must have been a mixture of shock and relief that made me go straight to sleep.

Early the next morning the door was swung open and a solicitor came in with two police officers. They asked me if I wanted to make a phone call and if I wanted to inform my parents. Good God no! I still thought, for some reason, that they were going to let me go home. I thought that once I got home I would put it all behind me and Mum and Dad need never find out. That was stupid, I know, but I wasn't thinking straight. It was like a nightmare that I couldn't wake up from.

I phoned my boyfriend and he came straight down to see me. I needn't have worried about telling my parents. They already knew. The village grapevine didn't waste any time. As soon as they heard, they came straight down to the police station along with my Aunt Marilyn. I was allowed to see them in a small, cold interview room. That was the first time I had ever seen my dad cry and it nearly broke my heart. They couldn't understand it and kept asking me: 'Why? Why?' But I couldn't answer them. I didn't know why myself.

Once Mum and Dad arrived, I thought that they would take care of it and tell the police that it was all a big mistake but it wasn't that simple.

I explained everything to my parents and the police. I told them I didn't know Scott Beaumont and I didn't know that he had been stabbed. Or rather I did know, but I didn't. It was all such a mess. I told them yes, I had got the knives in my pocket and yes, I did get them from my parents' shop but I never intended for anyone to be stabbed.

'But why did you take them?' They kept asking me over and over again.

'I don't know! I don't know! Just to frighten him, no, not to frighten him, just to, just to . . . I don't know, I can't explain.'

They questioned me for hours. Mum and Dad waited in the reception area for me. When the officer came in to charge me formally, he let Mum, Dad and Aunt Marilyn be with me. When he read the charge sheet out and said I was charged with murder, Mum and Dad started to cry. I was so frightened. I screamed at the officer: 'No, you're wrong! It must be a mistake! I haven't killed anyone!' But it was no mistake, and it was no dream.

Mum said, 'Don't worry, darling, it will all be sorted out soon.' She went on: 'When you go to court ...'

'Go to court?' I screamed. God, I didn't realise I would have to go to court. I asked the officer what had happened to my friends. He said that Kieron had been released. Beverley and Julie had been charged with violent disorder and Nicky and I were charged with murder.

Mum asked him what happened next. He said that I would be moved to Barnsley police station later that evening. Barnsley police station was attached to the Magistrates' Court and I would appear there on Monday morning.

I was put back in my cell to await transport to Barnsley. I couldn't believe this was happening. I still thought that at any minute someone would come in and say it was a mistake, but they didn't. After a meal of minced beef and mashed potatoes served on a small metal tray, an officer came in and handcuffed me to take me to Barnsley. As I walked into Barnsley police station, I was told to wait. To my surprise, Nicky, Bev and Julie were there and we were all put into a cell together. Nobody said a word; all the girlie chat had stopped. Overnight we had lost our youth – we were like strangers. We just sat there, quiet, shocked, stunned, deep in our own thoughts.

Early next morning officers came to take us into the

Magistrates' Court. The hearing was over in a matter of minutes. We were all remanded in custody. That didn't mean a thing to me. I had never been in trouble before. I had never been in a police station before, let alone a court. I hadn't a clue what 'remanded in custody' meant. I was put back in my cell and left to stew. An hour later, a policewoman came in and abruptly told me to get ready. 'You're going to Flockton,' she snapped.

'Flockton! Flockton! What the hell is that?'

'It's a prison,' she said. 'What do you think it is – Butlins?'

I turned to the others and asked, 'Why me?' A million questions were running around in my head. Why was I the only one going to prison? Why were they picking on me? I didn't want to go on my own. I wanted the others to come with me.

The solicitor came in and explained that I was old enough to go to prison but the others were too young. Bev and Julie were both remanded into the care of the local authority and taken to a children's home. Nicky was transferred to a secure unit in Liverpool and I was to be taken to Flockton Prison. I was handcuffed to a policewoman and put in the back of a police car. I was so scared. I didn't know what to expect. All the things that I had ever heard about prison came flooding into my mind.

I turned to the policewoman and started to cry: 'Will I be beaten up? Will they make me scrub the floor with a toothbrush?'

I was looking to her for a bit of reassurance but she just

looked out of the window at the rain and snapped, 'It's not the sort of place I would want to go. It's horrible, dirty.' She turned to face me and sneered, 'Whatever you do don't tell anyone what you're in for. Don't dare tell anyone that you're in for murder or they will beat you up.' I was terrified.

We drove up to the prison. I tried to peer through the window and get a better look. The windscreen wipers dragged slowly across the glass as they wiped away the drizzle from the windscreen. I could see the high walls and barbed wire. It looked so grey, so daunting. I tried to put my hands up to hide my eyes but the policewoman jerked the handcuffs down.

'Oh my God,' I cried. 'I want to go home! Please don't put me in here!' The big gates opened and the car drove in and it seemed like we were swallowed up.

At that moment I thought I would never survive and I would never get out of there. The police handed me over to an elderly female prison officer in reception and I was surprised that she was quite friendly. She told me not to tell any of the other girls that I was in for killing someone. As her eyes scanned my charge sheet, she smiled and said, 'Oh, I see, it was a man you did. Oh well, that's different.' She started to laugh, 'Maybe you can tell them, they won't mind so much, it being a man you killed.'

The officer looked at me and smiled. It was a vain attempt by her to make me feel a little better. She could see I was scared to death. I sobbed, 'I haven't killed anybody.' I wanted her to believe me, 'I haven't! Honest, I haven't!'

She just nodded and continued to tick endless bits of paper on her clipboard. It was all just a job to her. She must have seen thousands of prisoners come into prison and they all say the same thing: 'I'm innocent, Guv!' But this was my life, and I was innocent! I hadn't killed anyone!

I was taken to the hospital wing for assessment. It was just like being in any other hospital, only I was locked in. There weren't many girls in the hospital at that time, but I met a girl called Dawn. She was the same age as me and was also on a similar charge.

We were both frightened of what was going to happen to us so we decided to stick together. Over the next ten days, I was asked a million questions. All about my home life, my family, my friends. You name it, they asked me. In the end, they must have thought I was sane enough to be moved to the main wing of the prison. Me and Dawn stuck together all the time, like glue.

I soon learned that prison wasn't as hard as I thought it was going to be. My main fears were that I was going to be bullied or threatened and the other inmates would 'get me'. But they didn't. The older women helped me, took me under their wing, showed me the ropes. They told me who to talk to and who not to talk to. Dawn didn't stay long. She was transferred to a psychiatric hospital and when she went I missed her. I felt I was on my own now.

I didn't have a cell to myself. I was put on a dorm with a few other girls. I got a job in the kitchen and was told I would have to wait to appear in court. I was allowed to have four visits a week while I was on remand and Mum came up every visiting day, she never missed a visit. My mum is such a strong lady and she never doubted me for a moment. She pulled me through the endless court appearances. First they were every four weeks, then every two. Each time, I was remanded. Six months in all. When I was due up in court again, it was Friday 13 November 1992. It was yet another pre-trial review. I didn't want to go. I was sure it would be unlucky, being the thirteenth.

I was taken to court that morning and put in the cell as usual. I had become quite used to it over the past six months. My barrister came in to see me and told me he was going to put in an application for bail. I just went along with him but I didn't hold out much hope. The dock at Sheffield Crown court was a very frightening place. I stood up and my barrister hadn't said three words when the judge interrupted him and said, 'Yes, yes, bail granted.'

I couldn't believe it, I had got bail! I was going home! I started to cry and was taken back to my cell to wait for the papers to be sorted out. I waited for two long hours. I kept thinking they were going to come in the cell and tell me it was a mistake and that I couldn't go home.

Eventually, the prison officer who had brought me from Flockton came in. She was a nice lady, a very mumsy type. She had tears in her eyes and said, 'Come on, Avril, it's time to go. I hope everything works out for you and I don't want to see you again.' She unlocked the door and Mum was waiting for me. She opened her arms wide. I dropped my little bundle that I had under my arm and flew into my mum's outstretched arms.

Mum cried; so did I. I felt so safe in my mum's arms and she hugged me so tight I thought I was going to burst. I wanted that moment to last forever. I looked round and saw my aunt and cousin – they'd come to welcome me home. Mum grabbed my hand and said, 'Let's get out of here. Let's go home.'

I walked out of the court into the streets of Sheffield on that cold wet Friday morning in November. To feel the rain on my face and to be free again was the most marvellous feeling. They say you don't know what you've got until it's gone and they're right. Until I lost my freedom, I didn't realise how lucky I had been.

I had been away for six months. God knows what it's like for someone who has lost their liberty for 15–20 years. After just six months, just to walk down the street felt strange. The traffic seemed so noisy and so fast.

Mum had phoned Dad and told him I had got bail. As we pulled up outside our house, Dad came rushing out. He ran down the garden path and swept me off my feet. He couldn't say anything, he was crying so much. I felt so safe in my dad's big strong arms as he swung me round. I felt all the love and warmth oozing out of him.

The next call was to my grandma, she only lived down the hill. Mum said. 'I'd better go in first. If you walk straight in it might give her a heart attack.' Gran wasn't on the phone so Mum couldn't phone her and tell her I had got bail. I was her only grand-daughter and all this had upset her so much. I walked into her kitchen. She had been baking and the smell of bread wafted around the kitchen. It felt so familiar. Gran was sitting at the old pine table and her eyes aren't what they used to be. She looked up and said, 'Is that our Avril? It can't be.'

I knelt down and put my head on her lap and said, 'Yes, Gran, it's me.'

She stroked my hair and cried. 'Thank God, my baby's home.'

That was the happiest day of my life. I decided to make the most of the time I had on bail, before my trial. I went out with my friends and spent as much time with my family as I could. All the time, the trial date was looming. My trial was set for 21 June 1993. That seemed a long way off so I tried to blank it out of my mind, I thought it would never get here. I had eight long months of freedom and I was going to make the best of it but it wasn't all plain sailing.

During this time, I started to think about Scott, the lad that had been killed. I couldn't get him out of my mind. I wanted to know how he died. Did he die alone? It was on my mind day and night, not a day passed when I didn't think about him.

Julie and Beverley were also out on bail but in March 1993, just three months before our trial, Julie, Nicky's sister, was killed in a car accident. I was devastated. Julie's death affected me badly. I started to withdraw into a shell. I stopped going out and spent most of my time in my room. The trial was only three months away and I kept a calendar on my wall, in my bedroom, crossing the days off one by one. One month to go, then three weeks, two weeks, one week and then, before I knew it, it was the night before my trial. That night I went to bed early but I couldn't sleep. I just cried into my pillow. I was crying because I was scared; I was crying for Julie, I was crying for Scott, I was crying for my family; for just about everything.

Next morning Mum came into my room with a mug of tea. She sat on the edge of my bed. She dropped her head and fumbled with her hanky as she struggled to find the right words to comfort me. I felt so sorry for her. But she couldn't hide her emotions any longer. The tears welled up in her eyes as she sobbed, 'Don't be frightened, baby. You're going to be all right.' She nearly choked on the words as she said them.

We arrived at the court early. Sheffield Court House is an old-fashioned building. It's a daunting place with heavy oak panelling all around it. It has a raised dock with a heavy brass rail around it, and it smells musky, like an old church hall. From the moment I walked in I felt as though I was completely at the mercy of the legal people.

They were all there: the barristers, solicitors, QCs, the judge with his posh robes and wig. I couldn't follow any of the jargon. They spoke a different language to me. I felt helpless among all these people I had never seen before. They had my whole life in their hands.

I was led into court along with Nicky, Beverley and Kieron and the indictment was read out. Scott's family were there and sat on the opposite side to our family. I felt ashamed when I looked at their ashen faces. Witnesses came and went. People stood up and argued points of law. Every day the gallery was full of reporters scribbling on notepads. Our trial lasted 13 days. Eventually, the jury went out on the Tuesday morning to consider their verdicts on Nicky. On Tuesday afternoon they returned and Nicky was told to stand. I closed my eyes and prayed, 'Please, please don't let her be found guilty.'

I felt for her mum. She had already lost Julie. How would she cope if she lost Nicky too. Nicky just stood there. She looked like a little girl standing in the dock. You could have heard a pin drop as the foreman read out the verdict: 'Guilty!'

Nicky went white. All I can remember hearing is her mum cry out, 'No! No!'

The next day, Wednesday, it was Beverley and Kieron's turn. They were found not guilty. That gave me a bit of hope. They had been there just like I was and they had been found not guilty. On the Thursday morning it was my turn. I sat in the dock on my own with two Group 4 officers behind me. I was told to stand.

Everything seemed in slow motion. The whole court house was silent as the foreman said they could only reach a 10–2 majority verdict. The judge said he'd allow that. My eyes scanned the faces of the jury for some clue. I saw two lady jurors in the front crying. I knew then straight away it was bad news. The foreman said, 'Guilty of murder.'

I felt like the whole world had stopped. My world had ended. I had nothing left to live for, everything had gone. I couldn't take it. I was all alone. My head was swimming. I remember hearing a gasp go round the court, then I fell forward and banged my head on the shiny brass rail around the dock. The Group 4 officers picked me up and half carried me down to the cells. As they opened the door, I fell on the floor of the cell. I felt I had been drained of all my strength.

I remember there was a man in the cell waiting to go on trial for burglary and as I fell to the ground he said, 'What's happened?'

One of the Group 4 officers was called Mo. She was a smashing lady and had been with me throughout my trial. She was so upset. She said, 'She has been found guilty of murder, bless her heart.'

The man was horrified and said, 'How can they do that to her? She's only a kid!'

Mo and the man picked me up from the floor and laid me on the bed. Mo was crying. They tried to comfort me but what could they say? Everything was lost and they knew it. Nothing they could say could help. I had nothing left to live for. Then the word came; I was to go back up for sentencing.

The jury had asked to be excused. They didn't want to know the fate they had given me. Nicky and I stood in the dock and clung to each other as the judge said: 'You have been found guilty of the murder of Scott Beaumont. Sadly, there is no other sentence I can pass. You will be detained at Her Majesty's Pleasure. Take them down!'

My mum and auntie were allowed to come down to the cells with me. I had just passed my nineteenth birthday. I sat on my mum's lap and cried. I wanted to be five years old again. The screw came in and said Mum had to go. I pleaded with her not to leave me. She said she wanted to get home and tell Gran so she didn't see it first on the news. I knew she was right but I was scared. I held her tight and closed my eyes. 'Please, Mummy don't leave me.'

She got up and pulled away. 'I'm sorry darling, I've got to go.'

Richard John Dennick

Killers

The party revellers laughed and joked with the 22-year-old gate crasher who stood in the corner. They even gave him a drink. But then, they didn't know he was a dangerous escaped prisoner. Richard Dennick had been jailed for the 'evil' murder of a village rector and he had walked into the swinging party minutes after scaling the high stone walls of Lewes Prison in Sussex.

Six years earlier Dennick had stabbed a rector, Canon Alan Jones, through the heart. Now he was on the run after using a rope made of knotted blankets to escape from the prison hospital wing. Just before midnight he had scaled the four inner security walls, each 17 feet high.

Once out, Dennick ran as fast as he could for about a mile

before eventually stopping to catch his breath. Exhausted, he leaned against a wall and was instantly attracted to the sound of loud music coming from a party at a social club in the grounds of East Sussex Council headquarters.

Dressed only in an orange T-shirt and jeans, he quickly made his way to the party. Within minutes, the unshaven desperate prisoner was mingling freely with the hundred guests. They, thinking he was just a late arrival, gave him a tin of beer and made him feel welcome. He then boarded a coach with the partygoers and escaped to Brighton, where he ran off.

Then, after four months on the run, the killer was found again in Wormwood Scrubs, under the phoney name of Jason Ward. He'd been charged with possessing an imitation gun with intent to rob.

Dennick's life sentence began in March 1983 but his story begins six months earlier.

The kind old rector of Llanberis, Gwynedd, North Wales, Canon Alan Jones, 64, allowed the young boys of the village to use his rambling, ivy-clad home to meet in and play snooker. Richard Dennick, who was just 15 years old, and his friend Barry Boyle, aged 17, went to the rectory to play snooker. However, they also planned to rob the clergyman because they wanted money to run away to the bright lights of London.

In the big old games room, the two boys pretended to play snooker. All the time they were waiting to make their move. They hung around until everyone was gone. At last, they were alone in the house with the rector.

Using a broken billiard cue, a heavy metal ornament and a knife, they attacked him. Dennick struck the canon over and over again, with such ferocity that the brass ornament was twisted out of shape. Then, in the hallway, he found a large paperknife and drove it into the canon's head, collarbone, arm and finally, his heart.

While Dennick attacked the canon, Barry Boyle, half-scared out of his wits, fled from the rectory and phoned for an ambulance.

When the police arrived they found a boy kneeling by the rector's body. Blood was splattered everywhere. The boy sat motionless, covered in blood, his eyes glazed.

The jury took seven hours to find Dennick — the son of an army warrant officer — guilty. The judge, Mr Justice Mars-Jones, described him as 'evil' as he sentenced him to be detained during Her Majesty's Pleasure. Barry Boyle admitted assault with intent to rob and was sent to Borstal for six months.

Seven years later, Richard Dennick escaped from Lewes Prison in Sussex. He was on the run for six months. In February 1990 he was 'found' in Wormwood Scrubs under the false name of Jason Ward. Richard Dennick was sent back to a Category A prison to complete his life sentence. While there, the handsome 25 year old started to withdraw into himself. Slowly, he began to mistrust everyone around him. He started to spend hours alone, shut up in his cell, and his mind began to play tricks on him. He became more and more paranoid. Eventually, he was declared insane.

I first met Richard Dennick while he was in Lewes Prison, shortly before his escape. My brother-in-law Reggie had been moved from Gartree Prison to Lewes and had befriended Ricky. It was on one of my visits to see Reg that he introduced me to this tall baby-faced young man with ice-blue eyes and honey-blonde hair.

He was the spitting image of Steve Davis the snooker player. At the time Ricky was into painting and wanted to paint a portrait of me. After our visit he wrote to me and asked if I or Ron minded. Ron said he didn't mind but I didn't hear another word from Ricky. I never got the picture so I assumed that he had changed his mind.

Not long after that, early one morning, the police knocked on my door. Ricky had escaped. As I had been on the list of people whom he had written to, they had come to give my gaff a spin. I didn't mind. I had nothing to hide – especially not an escaped prisoner. After that I didn't hear anything of Ricky for a couple of years.

Then, late one afternoon, the phone rang. 'Hello, Kate, remember me? It's Ricky Dennick – I'm in Rampton. I'm working my ticket!'

Straightaway I knew what he meant. I'd heard the expression 'working my ticket' before. It means a prisoner has either gone mad or is faking being mad in order to get to one of the nut houses as they are generally known to be a bit more relaxed than prisons. I asked Ricky how he was and if he wanted to be a chapter in my book. He agreed.

It took me four hours to drive to Rampton Hospital. It's a big, daunting place but has an air of calmness about it. I was a bit apprehensive going in but the male nurse who lead me into the depths of Rampton's bleak corridors, chatted away.

At the entrance to Concord Ward, the nurse unlocked the heavy iron door and stood back to let me walk in.

Ricky was waiting for me. I hardly recognised him. The baby face had become lined and taut. His honey-blond hair was cut close to his head. He held his hand out and grinned. He moved towards me to say 'Hello'. His actions were slow and his speech was slightly slurred. I knew he was 'working his ticket' but he was not faking – he was obviously very ill.

We sat down and slowly he started to tell me the harrowing story of what had happened to him.

This is what Ricky told me.

★ ★ ★

I met Canon Alan Jones on the Monday – and I killed him on the Tuesday. I hated him. I knew within hours of meeting him I was going to kill him.

But, in fact, that Monday started normal enough, just like any other Monday. I was at my friend Barry's. I was lying on his bed, watching the snooker on his black and white TV. I love snooker, in fact everyone says I'm the spitting image of Steve Davis. As usual, we were bunking off school. It was pouring with rain and we were both fed up.

I had been sent to stay with my Aunt Frances, her husband Colin and their three-year-old son Gerrard in their small terraced house in Llanberis, North Wales. I liked my aunt, she was kind. I felt she liked me too. My parents had sent me to stay with her as a final resort. I was always a bit wild as a child. Every parent's nightmare. I was forever bunking off school, shoplifting and nicking cars. You name it and I did it. I think my parents just didn't know what to do with me next. So, for a well-earned break more than anything, I was sent to live with my aunt. I think in a way they were glad to see the back of me for a while.

My aunt was nice. She took time out to talk to me. I felt I could talk to her about almost anything, except what happened to me on 4 October 1982.

I was happy enough with my aunt. I settled down as well as can be expected. I even made a friend, Barry Boyle, who lived two doors away. Thinking back now, Barry was a slightly odd sort of a chap. He looked like a cross between John Lennon and Shaggy out of *Scooby Doo*. He loved The Beatles and always played their music loudly. Strangely, he always wore a brown-tweed, three-piece suit and he wore those little round glasses, just like John Lennon. All the kids in the village were wary of him but I didn't mind him. He was slightly older than me, 16.

Me and Barry would often bunk off school and doss around town but the small mining town in the depths of North Wales wasn't my idea of fun. I was bored. I needed excitement.

So when me and Barry was watching the snooker, I said to him, 'Let's nick a car and fuck off to London!'

Barry was all for it but we needed money. Barry said he had heard about this vicar that lived close by. 'He's a nonce!' Barry said. 'Likes boys! Let's go and rob the perv!'

I was 15 years old and a virgin. Sure, I knew what Barry meant when he said he was a 'nonce'. Or I thought I knew what it meant. Like most boys in his early teens, I was just discovering my sexuality. Barry flicked the telly off.

'Oi, I was watching that!' I snapped.

'Get your jacket,' he said. 'Lets go and suss out this pervy vicar!'

It was all a game at first. Me and Barry were larking about, screaming with laughter, making all sorts of jokes about monks and their dirty habits. But when we actually got to the old vicarage, we stopped laughing. It was a big rambling old house, set in its own grounds. We stood outside the tall iron gates.

Barry nudged me, 'You go first!'

'Fuck off – you go first!'

We made our way up to the big oak door and rang the bell. I half-expected an old butler to come to the door and say, 'You rang?', like you see in those old horror movies. The door creaked open and there stood a slightly balding, fat, bespectacled vicar, the Canon Alan Jones.

His eyes lit up when he saw us. 'Hello, boys – come in.'

We walked into the vestibule. The walls were covered with dark oak panelling and a huge polished staircase dominated the hall.

'Come to play snooker – like my other boys? Next time you come, use the back entrance,' he drooled.

From the moment he opened the door, his eyes were locked on me, watching my every move. He led us upstairs to the snooker room, taking every opportunity to touch me. At first he would just brush past me; then a hand on my shoulder or around my waist. He kept coming up close to me, saying suggestive things. He kept referring to my reddish hair and saying, 'Bet you got a big copper knob.' He wasn't very subtle and his bad breath made me want to vomit. I knew what he wanted – he wanted to fuck my arse.

On my way out, I noticed an ivory-handled paper knife on the table in the hallway. I grabbed it and stuffed it into my pocket. I took it with the sole purpose of killing the dirty bastard. I wanted him dead for what he wanted to do to me, and all the other boys before me. If I killed him then he wouldn't be able to hurt anyone else.

When I got home, I half-wanted to tell my aunt what that vile man had said but I couldn't find the right words. If only I hadn't gone to the vicarage. I felt in some ways it was my own fault. I felt dirty-sick. How could I explain to her that I had gone there to rob the vicar. I said nothing and went straight to my room. All night I lay on my bed. I couldn't sleep, I couldn't cry. I was numb. All I wanted to do was kill him.

The next day, Tuesday 5 October 1982 – my mum's birthday – my aunt called upstairs, 'You up yet, Ricky? You're going to be late for school!'

But I had been up for hours, plotting my revenge. I ran down the stairs and out the back door without saying a word. I sat on the wall outside Barry's house waiting for him. Barry slammed the door behind him. 'Fuck school, let's go down the town!' he mumbled, ramming a half-eaten piece of burnt toast into his mouth.

We wandered around Boots the chemist, I wanted to nick something for my mum's birthday but, instead, I ended up nicking some brown hair dye. God knows why? I suppose I still had it firmly set in my mind that I was going to 'do' that pervy vicar. We walked about aimlessly. I nicked some fags from a newsagents while I was buying *The Sun* newspaper.

I sat on the wall outside and read the story of a gangland murder committed by two brothers called Ronnie and Tony Par. Little did I know that five days later I would be sharing a cell with them.

I got back home just after 4.30 p.m. Auntie was humming away in the kitchen, busy cooking my tea. 'Egg, chips and beans do ya, Ricky?' she said. Little Gerrard climbed up on my lap. There was a parents' meeting that night at my school and she was going. The meeting started at seven and I was babysitting Gerrard. I didn't relish the task. He could be a right little sod and he always played me up.

I scoffed my tea down quick. I had things to do. I had arranged to meet Barry. We had planned to go to the vicarage and 'sort' the vicar. Auntie said I could go out but I had to be back by seven – no later.

Barry was waiting for me. He was excited. We had managed to get hold of the keys to an old Volkswagen car. 'We'll rob the vicar,' he said. 'Then we'll head for London'.

I told Barry: 'You can rob him if you like – I'm going to kill him!'

We arrived at the vicarage at 6.15 p.m. I banged on the door. To my surprise, a local kid answered the door. He couldn't have been any older than 14. 'Alan's out,' he said. 'Want a game of snooker?'

Me and Barry went upstairs and had a game. There was also three other boys there, playing snooker. Not long after, the vicar came back. He made a beeline straight for me. While the others chatted and played snooker, the reverend took me off to a quiet corner to have a chat.

I played up to him. I let him think that he could have his wicked way with me. His eyes looked right through me – undressing me. He never seemed to take his eyes off me, not for a moment. Not even to blink. His lips were wet and he had large dollops of white frothy spit in the corners of his mouth. He made me feel sick. He couldn't wait to get rid of the other boys. 'Come on boys, it's time to go,' he called.

Me and Barry held back and I closed and bolted the door behind the last boy. I handed the knife to Barry. 'Let's do him – let's kill the bastard now!'

The vicar came into the vestibule and took off his thick, heavy-rimmed glasses. He leered at me. 'Come on Ricky, come with me, I'll show you my special room. I call it my blue room'. The blue room was supposed to be used for conferences and the like but he used it for 'getting hold' of his boys. As we were passing a stand of old snooker cues, he pointed to them, bragging proudly, saying how 'long and thick' they were. His sexual innuendoes were disgusting and turned my guts.

I stopped at the rack of cues, took one off the stand and handed it to Barry. The reverend was walking through another door leading off the vestibule. I nodded to Barry and whispered, 'Give me the knife. You knock him out with the snooker cue and I'll stab him!'

Barry took the cue out of my hand and slowly crept up on the vicar. Crack! He bashed him hard on the head. I heard the thump and I was still standing in the vestibule. The vicar cried out, 'Oh, my God!' He was stunned but put up a fight with Barry, getting him in a head lock. Barry started shouting. Kicking and punching out, he struggled like mad and managed to pull away. He rushed straight past me, unbolted the door and ran.

The vicar came out of the store room. Blood trickled from his nose. He didn't say a word. He just stared at me. Only this time the look wasn't a look of lust. It was a look of shock.

I didn't say anything. I rolled up my sleeves. I wanted to kill him. I reached over and took another cue from the rack and lunged at him. I swung the cue, catching him on the forehead. I kept bashing and bashing him on the head. But he wouldn't go down and he tried to grab me.

I fell back against a small altar table with the reverend clutching my waist. As I fell back, I grabbed a big brass chalice that had been standing on a lace doily. I rammed it across his head and into his face. Blood splattered everywhere. His face was covered in blood. You could no longer make out his dog-collar. All the hurt and anger I felt rushed over my body. I just kept hitting him, bringing the chalice down on his head. This seemed to stun him but also spurred him into defending himself. He was a strong old bastard and grabbed my neck, squeezing it tight. It didn't